D0597661

Wall Street

THE STORY OF THE STOCK EXCHANGE

Books by Dorothy Sterling
With photographs by Myron Ehrenberg

SOPHIE AND HER PUPPIES

UNITED NATIONS, N. Y.

BILLY GOES EXPLORING

TREES AND THEIR STORY

INSECTS AND THE HOMES THEY BUILD

WALL STREET
The Story of the Stock Exchange

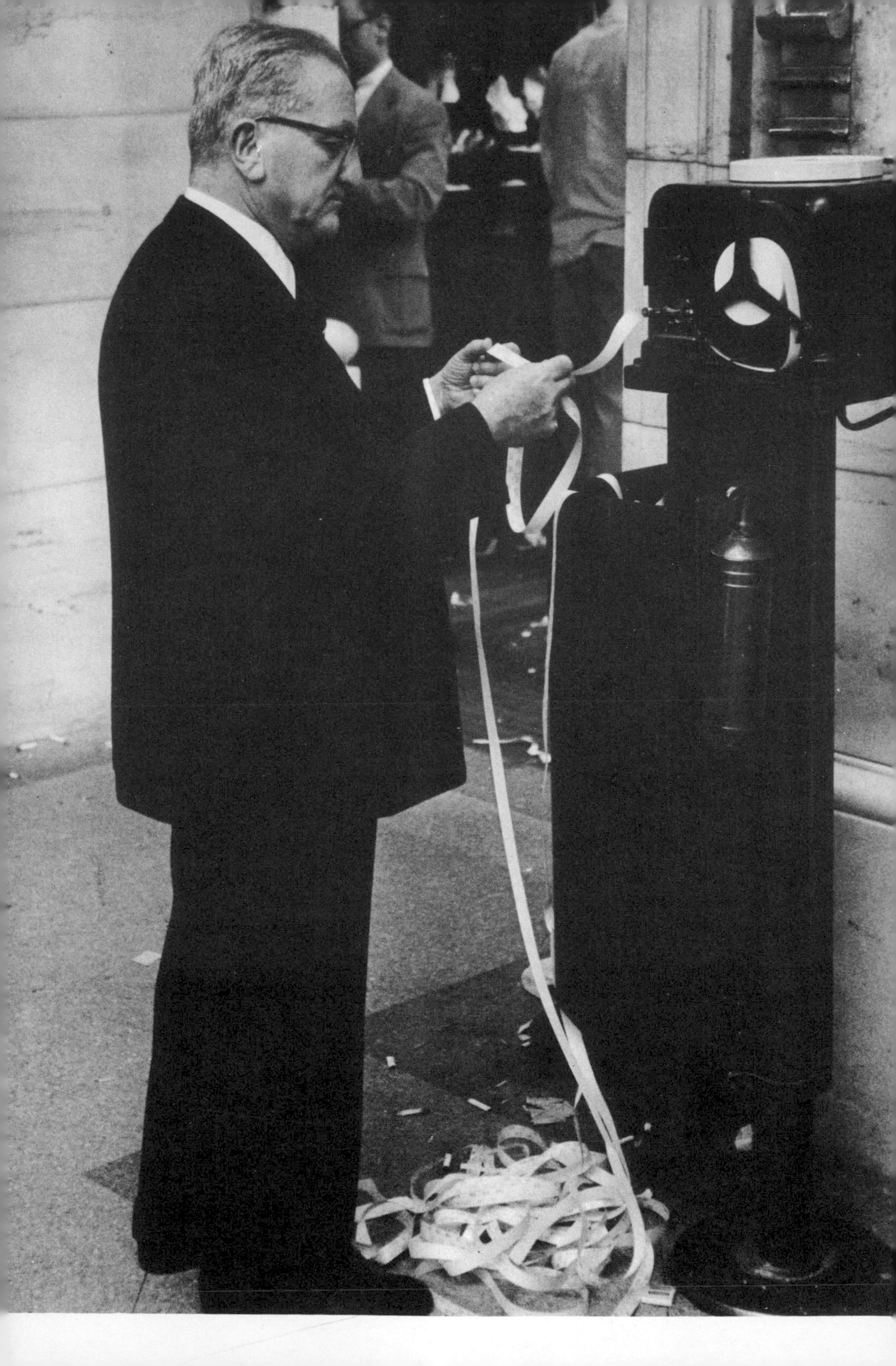

Wall Street

THE STORY OF THE STOCK EXCHANGE

By Dorothy Sterling

With Photographs by Myron Ehrenberg

DOUBLEDAY & COMPANY, INC., GARDEN CITY, NEW YORK, 1955

Library of Congress Catalog Card Number 55-9010
Lithographed in the U.S.A.

DEDICATION

To my father who told me
about the Stock Exchange in 1929

Acknowledgments: The authors would like to thank the New York Stock Exchange and the American Stock Exchange for permitting us to take pictures of their operations and for their many conscientious and courteous replies to our questions. The old pictures on pp. 28, 29, and 30 are from the files of the New York Stock Exchange; those on pp. 31, 36, 37, and 38 from the American Stock Exchange. The photographs on pages 14, 15 and 16 were taken at the Chase Museum of Money, the photograph on page 26 at the New York Historical Society.

CONTENTS

Wall Street

THE STORY OF THE STOCK EXCHANGE

Barter

CHAPTER 1 About some words

Money is a copper penny and the dime that buys an ice cream cone. Money is a dollar earned for baby-sitting or cutting the neighbor's grass. Money is to save for a new bicycle. Money is to spend for a new dress.

Money is what buys things. It seems simple to understand. But money is complicated too. You can earn it and spend it. You can borrow it and lend it. You can save it and invest it.

You can use money to buy a pair of shoes or to build machinery with which to make thousands of pairs of shoes. Or you can invest it in the business of a shoe manufacturer. Money changes its name, depending on the use to which it is put. Money is *wages*. Money is *savings*. Money is *capital*.

The study of what happens to money and how it is used is part of a science called *economics*. In order to express economic laws and theories in precise terms, scientists sometimes use long words and jaw-breaking phrases. Don't let these frighten you.

You've been studying economics since the day you traded your red fire truck for Tommy's cap pistol or Anne's mama doll. When you give two Yankee baseball cards for a picture of Jackie Robinson or exchange a stamp in the presidential series for the first Coronation issue, you're following time-honored business methods. Maybe you can't define laissez faire or explain the law of diminishing returns, but every time you plunk down a quarter at the ticket window of a movie theater you're engaging in a kind of high finance that your ancestors would have marveled at.

Way back in the days of the cave men and the tree dwellers, there was no such thing as money. The bears and deer which Papa killed were turned into food and clothing by Mama and the children. Each family produced only for its own needs and used all that it could produce. There was nothing for people to exchange.

Then Mama experimented with scratching the earth with a stick and planting the seeds of wild grasses while Papa discovered that some of the animals he hunted could be tamed and milked and bred. Alongside the hunters, tribes of farmers and herdsmen sprang up. With this first division of labor, there were goods to be exchanged.

You recognize this kind of business dealing. Exchanging bearskins for grain, deer meat for goats' milk, is not very different from trading stamps and baseball cards or exchanging a cinch belt for a scarf. You call it swapping. The economists' name for it is *barter*.

After the discovery of farming, invention followed upon invention. Clay pots and bowls, looms for weaving cloth, bronze tools and weapons, wooden wheels. In this new world of manufactured goods, barter was not always practical. Farmer Hammurabi wanted a bronze ax. Metalworker Rameses needed a new wheel for his cart, and Mrs. Ptolemy, wife of the wheelwright, was fresh out of grain for the family bread.

Gradually a new trading system was worked out. Some one thing had to be found that each of them would be willing

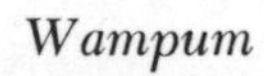
Wampum

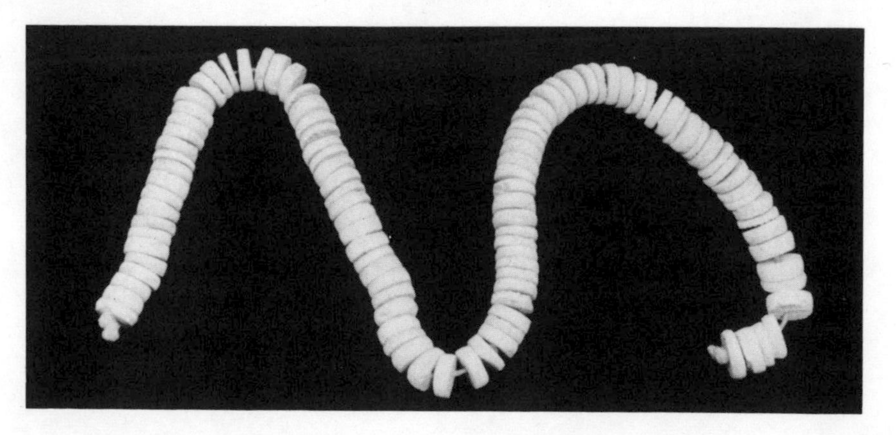

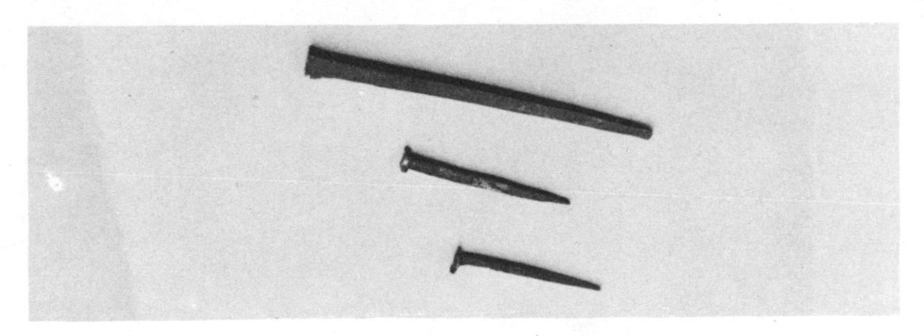

Handmade Iron Nails

to accept in exchange for their goods. For a pound of salt, Farmer Hammurabi could have Rameses' bronze ax. A half pound of salt bought the sack of grain for the Ptolemys. Two pounds of salt were traded for the spokeless wheel for Rameses' cart. Salt was the product that each was willing to accept in exchange. The value of the ax, the grain, and the wheel was figured in pounds of salt. Salt was money.

Money took different forms in different parts of the world. Goods could be exchanged for cattle, animal skins, dried fish, soap, coal, jewelry. In some countries gold and silver, measured by the ounce, changed hands freely. In others, copper slabs and iron bars were carted to the market place. Metal coins circulated in China in the seventh century B.C., but two thousand years later they were still unknown in North America.

Even in colonial times, only prosperous merchants jingled Spanish pieces of eight or English shillings in the pockets of their pantaloons. Most Americans used the kinds of money pictured on these pages. The wampum necklace is made of seashells that the Indians carved and strung together. Six of the shell beads were exchangeable for an English penny. Handmade iron nails were common currency in New England, while in Virginia the early settlers made their purchases with tobacco.

Fur trading was big business, and a port city like New Amsterdam reckoned in terms of beaver skins. One soft brown pelt would buy four pecks of peas, two pints of gunpowder,

Beaver Skin

or a shirt. For a shirt with ruffles or a dozen knives, two pelts were needed. The value of all other furs was measured by the beaver. A bearskin equaled a beaver; so did two foxes or eight minks.

But the beaver money of New Amsterdam is far ahead of our story. The Age of Bronze in which Farmer Hammurabi and his friends lived was followed by the Age of Iron. With iron axes, broad stretches of forest were cleared. With iron plowshares, small landholdings grew into great farms. The iron sword played its part in war and conquest. Stone and brick houses were built. Roads were cut through the mountains, and ships sailed the seas with cargoes for other lands.

The wealth of the world increased a thousand times, and a thousand times again. No longer was each family producing only enough for a bare existence or trading its meager surplus with its neighbors. Now there were new divisions among peoples. Rich men and poor, kings and commoners, free and slave. Farmer, artisan, merchant.

The farmer in the country did not trade directly with the metalworker in the walled city. His grain was sold to the merchant. His tools were purchased from the merchant. The merchant was the *middle man,* buying from those who produced goods, selling to those who consumed them.

In the hands of the merchant, money became more than just a convenient way of exchanging goods. It acquired new names and new uses. The merchant sold the farmer's grain and the metalworker's tools for a higher price than he paid for them. The difference between his costs and his selling price was his *profit.* Profits could be spent or saved, or used to make more profits.

Merchant Augustus loaned his savings to the wheelwright. Merchant Cicero purchased land outside the city. Merchant Marius bought a new loom for the weaver. Augustus received *interest* from the wheelwright for the use of his money. The farmer paid *rent* to Cicero for the use of his land. The weaver gave Marius a *share* of his earnings in return for the new loom. The merchants' savings had become *capital.*

With the invention of the sailor's compass, the earth grew larger—and smaller. New trade routes were explored, new lands discovered, and there was a new use for capital. An expedition around the Cape of Good Hope or across the wide Atlantic was too costly for one man to finance. Groups of merchants pooled their resources to outfit ships for these voyages. Each owned a share in the enterprise and divided the profits. Their organizations were *corporations.*

Our country was settled by the merchants' corporations of Europe: the London Company in Virginia, the Dutch West India Company in New York, the Massachusetts Bay Company in New England. Even the Pilgrims, seeking religious freedom, were financed by London merchants, for whom they agreed to work for seven years.

Opening up the new continent was a job for the ax and the plow and the rifle of the huntsman. While European investors received their profits in furs and lumber, in cotton and tobacco, most colonists were farmers, producing for their household needs. Bread was baked in the family fireplace, clothing woven on the family loom. Only an occasional peddler with a pack of pins and knives or an assortment of bone buttons carried on trade with the frontier families.

All machinery depended for its power on water and wind and the muscles of men. Then came the steam engine, perfected just seven years before the Declaration of Independence was signed, and life changed rapidly in both Old World and New. Sailing ships and stagecoaches gave way to steamboats and railroads. Coal was dug from the hills, steel rolled in the valleys, and the telegraph carried news of the discovery of oil.

Even faster than in the Age of Bronze and the Age of Iron, invention followed upon invention. The telephone and the electric light. The automobile and the airplane. The motion picture and the radio. Machines to plow the land and harvest the crops. Machines to flatten mountains and scoop out lakes. Even thinking machines, electric brains to solve mathematical problems that might take a man with a pencil one hundred years to figure out.

Soon the spinning wheel in the parlor grew dusty and the windmill stood idle in the fields. Production was moving from the home and the small shop to the factory. With a power loom, a woman could weave a hundred yards of cloth a day. With ten looms, ten women could weave a thousand yards. Chains of factories employing millions of workers now sprawl across the land.

These factories produce enormous quantities of goods for exchange—and require enormous sums of money to finance. Before the Civil War, most American businesses were small. They were owned by one man or one family. In the next decades, the situation was completely reversed. By 1900, three quarters of all U.S. manufactured goods were produced in factories owned by corporations.

Think about what these figures mean. Back in 1850, if Thomas Winthrop wanted to start manufacturing cotton sheeting, he could borrow money from family and friends or the local banker to pay for spindles and looms and a frame building to house them. Today he would need not thousands but millions of dollars for his machines and factory buildings. This is too much money to borrow in his home town. He must sell shares in his business, not only to neighbors, but to investors in Chicago, in New Orleans, in San Francisco and Providence.

The modern corporation is patterned on the old merchants' trading company, but it is infinitely bigger and more complicated. The London Company of Virginia was owned by a few hundred men. It spent a million dollars to establish a settlement in the New World. The American Telephone & Telegraph Company has 1,307,000 shareholders, and its plants and equipment are valued at $14,000,000,000.

Raising capital for American Telephone & Telegraph and its fellow giants has become a business in itself. In place of the merchant, there is the financier, the investment banker, the stockbroker. In their hands, a new kind of trading developed—the buying and selling of shares in industry.

To understand how this works, let's imagine that you want to start a lemonade stand. This is to be a super-stand, open every weekend all summer long. A real business.

Your mother groans, "I know you made a dollar and a half in one afternoon last year, but think of what it cost me in lemons and sugar and broken glasses. Don't count on me for your supplies!"

Perhaps John's mother or Joan's will have shorter memories. But Mrs. Brown reminds you of a borrowed pitcher that was returned without a handle, and Mrs. Smith needs the bridge table that you counted on for a stand.

"I can see we're going to have to finance this ourselves,"

you announce. "I have $2.00. How about the rest of you?"

"Only $1.00." John shakes his head.

"I have $3.00," Joan says, "but I don't know if I want to risk it all. Let's figure out what we'll need."

The three of you make a list. Lemon squeezer, pitcher, paper cups, sugar, lemons, table, cardboard for a sign. These are your tools and raw materials. The table will serve as both factory and store. Capital needed, $6.00, you calculate.

"Better make it $10," John suggests. "We'll need extra money to start off with, for making change."

"And in case we hit a rainy spell," Joan agreed.

Ten dollars is more than the three of you can scrape together. It will take weekends of odd jobs to save it up—warm weekends when you might profitably be selling lemonade. Maybe you can borrow it from other boys and girls in the neighborhood.

But when you talk to would-be investors, you're surprised to find suspicion, if not downright distrust. Even the younger children ask, "What's in it for me?" or "When will I get my money back?"

Tools and Raw Materials

Remember the modern Mr. Winthrop who couldn't borrow the capital he needed for his cotton mill? He solved his problem by selling shares in his business, asking strangers as well as friends to invest. You can do the same thing, your father points out.

Lemonade, Inc. is the answer. To raise the $10, you decide to issue 30 shares of stock at 25 cents a share, and 5 bonds at 50 cents each. Every stockholder is part owner of the business. At the end of the summer he will receive a portion of the profits, depending on the number of shares he owns.

"Those are your dividends," your father explains. "If you make $30 profit, you can pay a dividend of $1.00 a share. Then Joan, who owns 10 shares, will make $10. Now if anyone asks, 'What's in it for me?' tell them about the dividends."

The bonds are for the most cautious investors, the ones who say, "But suppose there are no profits?" or "When will I get my money back?" Each bond is a promise to repay the 50 cents on the day after Labor Day, with 5 cents interest. Bondholders aren't part owners of the company, nor do they share in its profits. They lend their money for a definite period of time, at a fixed rate of interest. They must be paid first, before the stockholders get their dividends. Their chance for profits is small, but so is their risk.

The boys and girls who wouldn't lend you $1.00 are glad to buy shares of stock for a quarter or spend 50 cents for a bond. In three days you've sold your entire issue. Lemonade, Inc., with eight stockholders and four bondholders, is in business.

And it looks like a good business. Hot, dry weather is on your side and your biggest problem is keeping the younger stockholders from dipping into the sugar. Your biggest problem, that is, until Joan smashes up her bike.

"It's going to cost $5.00 to repair," she reports," and Dad says I have to pay for it myself. You'll have to buy back my stock."

"But, Joan," you argue, "without your $2.50, we'll hardly have enough money for next week's lemons."

"Or for a rainy day," John adds.

Peter, owner of two shares of stock, enters the discussion. "I'll buy your stock, Joan. Give you $2.00 for it."

"Two dollars!" Joan is horrified. "I paid $2.50 for it, and besides, I expect dividends. That's not fair."

Peter shrugs his shoulders. "If we run into rainy weather, there won't be any dividends. Better take the $2.00."

Judy has been doing some figuring. "I think Lemonade, Inc. is going to make money. I'll give you $2.50, Joan."

John and you check the contents of your pockets. "We'll make it $2.60," you announce.

"Two-seventy!" Peter tops your offer with a grin.

"Two-eighty," Judy says.

"Sold to Judy," Joan shouts triumphantly. "Ten shares for $2.80."

The two girls walk off, arm in arm, to exchange stock certificates and money. They have been buying and selling stocks, trading Joan's shares of ownership in Lemonade, Inc. for Judy's savings. Joan has made a profit by selling her stock for thirty cents more than she paid for it. Judy hopes to make a profit from the corporation's dividends.

It's easy for the stockholders of Lemonade, Inc. to meet and arrange to buy and sell their shares. There are only twelve shareholders, and they all live within a mile of each other. But when you multiply the twelve by 10,000—or 100,000, as is the case with American Telephone & Telegraph—the exchange becomes more difficult. Corporation directors and shareholders cannot conveniently meet and bargain face to face. Instead, they delegate the job to middle men, who do the buying and selling for them.

These middle men, these merchants-of-shares-of-ownership-in-industry, are financiers, investment bankers, and stockbrokers. They bring together corporations in search of capital and prospective shareholders in search of investment. They

make it possible for buyers to buy and sellers to sell. They represent traders in Chicago, in Alabama, in California and Maine.

Just as you can go to a market to buy a pound of hamburger or a dozen oranges, so you can go to a market to buy shares in a corporation that manufactures television sets or mines uranium. This is the *securities market*, which, when it is organized under one roof and closely regulated by law and custom, is called a *stock exchange*.

CHAPTER 2 The Wall becomes the Street

Headquarters for the American securities market is a narrow New York street, little more than a third of a mile long, whose story goes back to the days of the Dutch West India Company. It was 1644 when the Governor of New Amsterdam called on the citizens of the colony to build a barricade across the northern boundary of their settlement. From the river on the east to the Broad Way on the west, a barrier of trees and branches was constructed—"sufficiently strong to prevent the straying of cattle"—and to protect the village from Indian attack.

When war broke out between the Dutch and the English nine years later, the cattle barrier was replaced by a sturdy wall, a crisscross of wooden posts and boards, reinforced by ditches and sloping dirt breastworks. Its builders were paid for their labor in good wampum.

For fifty years the wall stretched across Manhattan Island. In times of peace its posts were burned for firewood. When war threatened, the stockade was hastily built up again. Through the Water Poort gate (lettered "M" in the picture on page 26) farmers from Haarlem and Breuckelen carried sacks of corn and traders brought their furs to the waterfront markets. Each night at nine, when the bell-ringer made his rounds, the gate was locked. Each morning at sunrise it was opened again.

After New Amsterdam became New York, the colony spread northward through the forests of Manhattan. The wall was torn down and a wagon road, thirty-six feet wide, laid out in its place. The rough dirt road was bounded on the west by the tall wooden steeple of Trinity Church. Close by, stones from the base of the old wall formed the foundations of a new City Hall. Here the Common Council met. Here were the

1949

'all Street

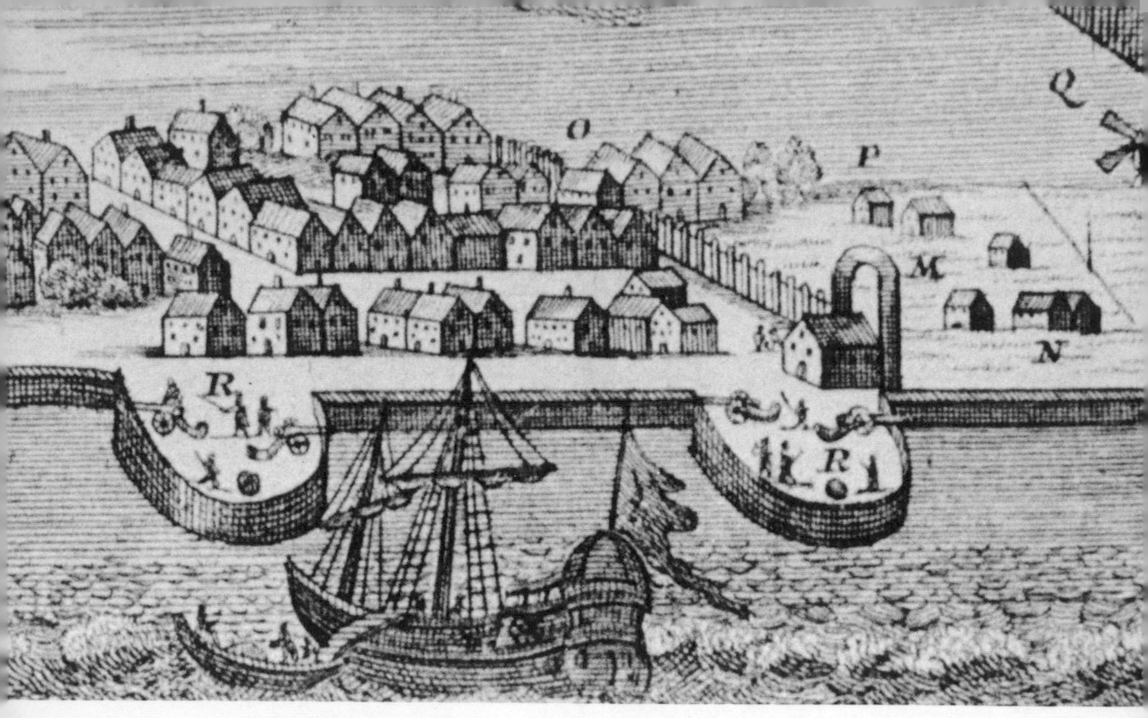

New Amsterdam's Wall

courthouse and jail, the library and fire department, while across the way stood stocks and pillory and whipping post. The homes of English gentry fronted on the road as it twisted toward the river. At the water's edge stood the Meal Market, where merchants traded in grain and Negro slaves. Beyond was the ferry to Long Island.

Through colonial times the road that followed the course of the old Dutch wall was one of the main thoroughfares of the city. While produce-laden wagons rumbled along its cobblestones to the markets on the wharves, the Stamp Act Congress assembled in City Hall and resolved to buy no more goods carrying the tax stamp of the English King.

Laid in ruins by the British occupation during the Revolution and a disastrous fire, Wall Street came to life again when the treaty of peace was signed. For five years it was the site of the capital of the new nation. City Hall became Federal Hall, and from its balcony Washington took the oath of office as first President of the United States. He lived nearby, in Fraunces Tavern, and on Sundays he worshiped in Trinity Church.

The capital moved from New York as part of a deal that was to make Wall Street the nation's financial center. The Revolution had thrown the country deeply into debt. In 1776, there was no national treasury, no American banks, no money for uniforms and food, for ammunition and soldiers' pay. The Continental Congress solved its problem temporarily by printing paper money, by loans from abroad, and by the sale of bonds marketed through loan offices to patriotic citizens.

After the war came the reckoning. No interest had been paid on loans or bonds, and there were dozens of different moneys—shillings, doubloons, gold, counterfeit—in circulation. The Continental dollars were worth only pennies in coin. Shops were papered with these bills, suits of clothes made from them, and "not worth a Continental" was a phrase on every man's lips.

Secretary of the Troasury Alexander Hamilton had the job of restoring business life. He proposed to combine all the obligations of the federal and state governments into one vast debt and to set about paying it off with money raised through taxes and duties on imported goods. This "funding of the debt" meant that all bond owners would turn in their old, worthless certificates and receive in exchange new bonds paying three and six per cent interest.

This practical-sounding solution met with a storm of opposition. Most of the patriotic citizens who loaned money to the wartime government no longer owned their bonds. In the lean post-war years speculators had bought up their certificates, paying only a few pennies for each dollar of the bonds' value. The speculators rather than the original purchasers of the bonds would benefit from Hamilton's proposal. Futhermore, while import duties would help manufacturers and businessmen in the North, they would be only an additional burden for hard-pressed farmers and Southern planters.

Hamilton's plan seemed slated for defeat until Thomas Jefferson engineered a compromise. Fearful of a split in the Union, he convinced Southern congressmen to vote for the

Sidewalk Stock Exchange

funded debt if the Northerners, in return, would move the nation's capital to the South. The seat of the government traveled to Philadelphia and then to the banks of the Potomac River—and traders bought and sold federal bonds on the newly paved sidewalks of Wall Street.

Trading was not new to the tangle of streets of downtown Manhattan. From the days of the Dutch, auctioneers had fanned out from the waterfront markets, selling bargeloads of wheat, bales of tobacco, cotton, and sugar and human lives. From roadside stands they hawked their goods, while passers-by stopped to listen and join in the spirited bidding.

It did not matter to these lusty-voiced merchants whether they sold groceries or government bonds. Their profits were based on the commissions they were paid for their sales. If there were customers for federal bonds or for the shares now being issued by Hamilton's Bank of New York and the new United States Bank, they were glad to trumpet the worth of the new securities.

Two years after the capital had been transferred from its

Wall Street home, there were skirmishes between the auctioneers and a new group of men who had begun to specialize in the buying and selling of stocks and bonds. The auctioneers announced public sales of securities each day at noon in front of Federal Hall. The stockbrokers set up their own headquarters, under the branches of a buttonwood tree farther down the street. Boycotting the auctioneers, they agreed to trade only with each other at a fixed commission rate.

Stockbrokers' Agreement, 1792

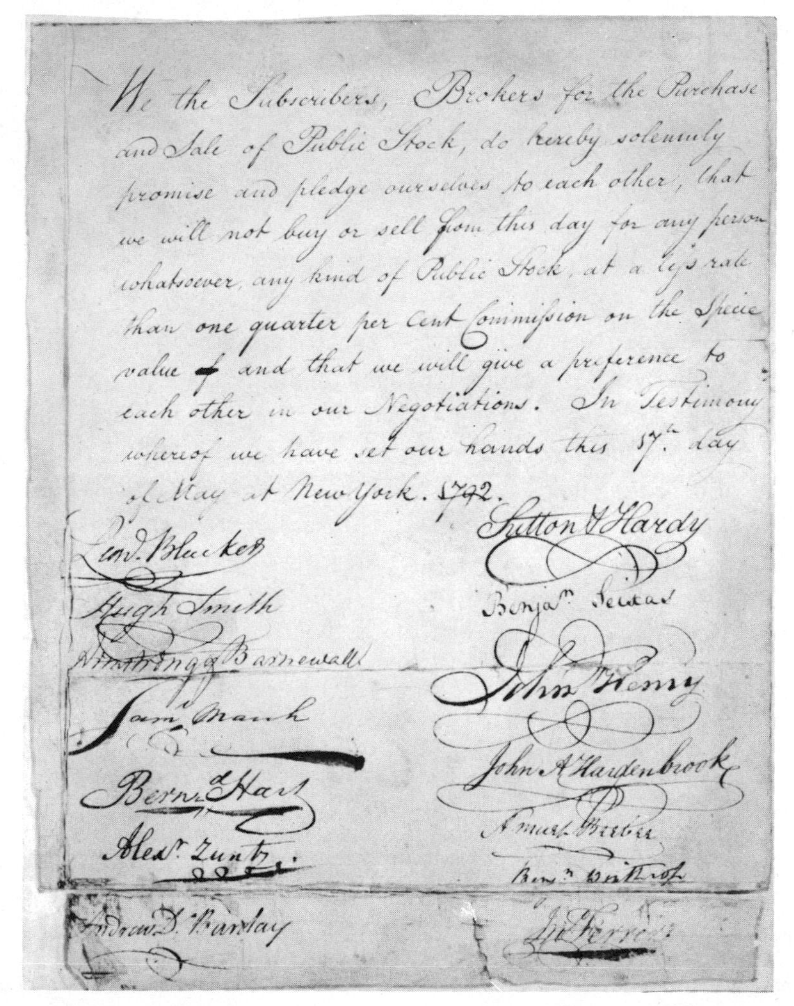

We the Subscribers, Brokers for the Purchase and Sale of Public Stock, do hereby solemnly promise and pledge ourselves to each other, that we will not buy or sell from this day for any person whatsoever, any kind of Public Stock, at a less rate than one quarter per Cent Commission on the Specie value of and that we will give a preference to each other in our Negotiations. In Testimony whereof we have set our hands this 17th day of May at New York. 1792.

Lend. Bleecker
Hugh Smith
Armstrong & Barnewall
Sam Marsh
Bernd. Hart
Alexr. Zuntz
Andrew D. Barclay

Sutton & Hardy
Benjan. Seixas
John Henry
John A. Hardenbrook
Saml. Beebe
Benjn. Winthrop
Jno. Ferrers

The Stock Exchange in 1850

As you can see from the picture on page 28, Wall Street in 1792 was very different from the wagon road of a century earlier. It was now a street of fashionable homes and shops. Hamilton lived on Wall Street, and his Bank of New York, the city's only bank, was located a few doors west of the buttonwood-tree market.

The dignified top-hatted gentlemen who fixed their signatures to the agreement on page 29 soon moved their business indoors, at first to a nearby coffeehouse, and then to a room of their own at 40 Wall Street. By 1817 they were formally organized, with constitution and membership rules, under the name of the New York Stock & Exchange Board.

In the early days of the Republic, trading in securities was not a big business. Sales at first were limited to government bonds and the stocks of banks and the new insurance companies. There was a flurry of activity during the War of 1812, when the government again needed financing. Soon afterward, forward-looking investors bought stock in the Erie

Canal and the turnpikes and toll bridges which were beginning to link coastal cities with the settlements along the Western frontier. But sales were small and the record books report a dull day in 1830 when only 31 shares changed hands—five shares of the Morris Canal and Banking Company and 26 shares of the United States Bank.

This was the year, however, that marked a turning point in the life of the securities market. The Tom Thumb, first American-made locomotive, puffed along the rails from Baltimore. It was followed by the Best Friend in South Carolina, and the railroad boom was on. Like the clipper ships that sailed the Atlantic in the sixteenth and seventeenth centuries, railroads were too costly for one man to finance. By 1835, shares in 23 railroads were sold in the rooms of the New York Stock & Exchange Board. Before the Civil War, member brokers were buying and selling 70,000 shares in a single day.

The picture on page 30 shows the Board in the 1850s, when it occupied spacious quarters in the Merchants' Ex-

Street-Corner Stock Market after the Civil War

change Building at 55 Wall Street. The members were grouped around long tables, each seated in a wooden armchair which he owned. At half-past ten every morning and at two-thirty in the afternoon, the president rose to read the list of stocks in which trading was permitted. As he called out each name, he paused to ask, "Any bids, gentlemen?"

From their seats, brokers shouted their bids to buy and offers to sell. When two of them agreed on a price, a sale was made and stock certificates and money changed hands before the following day. There were no written contracts.

Behavior in the Board room was strictly regulated. In the 1830s, members were fined a dollar if they threw paper darts. By 1870, the same offense cost $10, and there was a fine of $5.00 for smoking a cigar!

Operating behind closed doors, the Board permitted neither rival brokers nor the public to attend its sessions. Membership was a prized possession and only a few new brokers were admitted each year. The price for a seat on the Exchange rose steadily, from $25 in 1820 to $400 in 1837, until it reached $1,000 before the Civil War.

The railroad boom was paralleled by a rash of land speculation in the 1830s. Then came the gold rush to California and the speculative fever of the Civil War. There was money to be made by trading in stocks, and sales were no longer confined to the seventy-five gentlemen who sat in the decorous Board room. Rival exchanges sprang up and street-corner markets often did more business than the indoor traders. In the afternoon, when the Exchange had closed its doors for the day, even its own brokers joined the speculators outdoors and took part in the frenzied bidding.

Stock prices soared upward and tumbled downward and each boom ended in a crash which brought with it a wave of business failures. The Exchange weathered these, absorbing many of its rivals or joining forces with them. By 1869, it had become the New York Stock Exchange, with a membership of 1,060 and a building of its own, close to the corner of Wall

The New York Stock Exchan

NEW YORK STOCK EXCHANGE

Ceiling of the Trading Floor

Clock in Board of Governors' Room

and Broad streets. One hundred and forty-five stocks and 162 bonds were sold on the Exchange, with 50,000,000 shares changing hands each year.

The growth of the securities market continued to reflect the growth of the nation's business. Railroad stocks dominated trading until, in the 1890s, shares of gas, electric, and telephone companies were offered for sale. Then came the big industrial corporations: Standard Oil, United States Steel, General Motors. World War I introduced the "War Brides"—chemicals, munitions, copper, transport—the industries experiencing a wartime boom. Before 1914, Europeans had invested large sums of money in American securities. By 1918, the situation was reversed and Americans were buying foreign stocks and trading in them on the New York Stock Exchange.

The Broad Street home soon became too small, and in 1903 the Exchange moved to its present headquarters, a handsome white marble building, decorated with Grecian columns and a sculptured pediment whose figures symbolize American commerce and invention. Additional property was acquired in 1923 and 1928. Today the Exchange buildings spread over two thirds of a city block on Wall and Broad streets.

Although the buildings have been remodeled to permit the installation of modern equipment for high-speed communication, the Exchange clings to tradition in its architecture and decoration. The ceiling of the trading floor, one of the largest rooms in the world, is still covered with wreaths and curlicues and the brightest of gold paint. In the spacious committee room where the Board of Governors meets, a clock in its polished wood case ticks off the minutes, as it has done since 1867, when it was first installed on the trading floor.

While the Stock Exchange was acquiring the dignity that comes with age, the outdoor market also continued to grow. The street trading which had begun with the funding of the debt of the Revolution and had become frantic during the Civil War was called a *curb market*. Anyone could be a curb broker if he had strong lungs and would stand outdoors in

The Curb Market

rain or snow or broiling sun. Early in the twentieth century a group of men who had survived both inclement weather and financial crises organized this outdoor trading into the Curb Exchange. Although they still worked outdoors, they limited their membership and drew up a formal list of securities to be traded.

Crowding the sidewalks and spilling over into the streets, the Curb Exchange was for many years both a traffic hazard and a spectacle for sight-seers. The brokers, as you can see in the pictures, wore gaudy caps, sun helmets, and even green derbies so that their clerks, stationed on the lower floors of nearby buildings, could recognize them. Orders to buy and sell securities reached the clerks by telephone. They passed them on to the brokers through whistles, shouts, and an elaborate alphabet of hand signals.

Wartime prosperity finally put an end to the outdoor market. In 1921, the Curb brokers moved into a building of their own on Trinity Place, overlooking the graveyard of the old church. Their organization is now the American Stock Exchange, the second largest securities market in the United

Curb brokers bid for stocks

States. Despite its new headquarters and new name, brokers and clerks still use hand signals on the trading floor, and no Wall Streeter calls the exchange anything but "the Curb." Just as the New York Stock Exchange is still known as "the Big Board," from the days when it was the Stock & Exchange Board, and Wall Street is always referred to as "The Street."

History is a living thing on the southern tip of Manhattan Island, and traditions die slowly. The geography of the area is a constant reminder of colonial days. At lunchtime, office workers stroll along Beaver Street or Gouverneur Lane or Bowling Green, roads and park laid out by Dutch burghers and the English colonists who succeeded them. In the spring they sun themselves in Trinity churchyard, where a stone monument marks the 150-year-old grave of Alexander Hamilton.

Bankers and brokers lunch at Fraunces Tavern, restored by the Sons of the Revolution so that it looks just as it did when George Washington lived there. The wigged doorman who checks diners' hats and coats wears the uniform of a colonial coachman.

Curb broker signals to clerk

Across the street from the Exchange, Federal Hall still stands. For many years a Customs House and Sub-Treasury Building, it is now the Federal Hall Memorial Museum, with a statue of George Washington on its steps, marking the spot where he became our first President. You can see this statue in the foreground of the picture on page 33.

Today stone and steel skyscrapers thrust upward, shutting off the sun from the sidewalks below, making the narrow streets seem narrower. One hundred thousand people work in the financial district, buying and selling shares in industry—steel and automobiles, television and uranium. Together they handle twice as much money in a year as the United States Government does. But Wall Street—The Street—still winds from Trinity Church to the wharves at the river's edge, the width of a wagon road, following the course of the old Dutch wall.

Fraunces Tavern

Alexander Hamilton's Grave

The man who owns a seat on the Exchange

CHAPTER 3 A super-market

Consider some figures for a moment. More than $275,000,000,000 worth of stocks and bonds are listed for trading on the New York Stock Exchange. The corporations whose shares are bought and sold there produce three quarters of all U.S. automobiles and trucks, three quarters of our electric power, seven eighths of our finished steel. They refine 90 per cent of the country's oil, handle 90 per cent of domestic railroad and airline traffic. They make your breakfast cereal and soap, your candy bars and drinks, your movies and television programs.

An overwhelming percentage of the nation's business is represented in the buildings at the corner of Wall and Broad streets. Yet, despite the millions of dollars changing hands there every day, the New York Stock Exchange's profit in 1954 was only $33,000.

Does this sound strange? The explanation is a simple one. The Exchange itself is not primarily a profit-making organization. It does not buy or sell securities or fix their prices. It is a market place, where buyers and sellers meet and trade.

Maybe there's a Swap Shop in your town—a store where you can sell your outgrown skates and buy skis or hiking boots that a neighbor no longer uses. The Swap Shop does not set the price of the skates and skis. It merely offers counters and shelves for the display of merchandise.

On a larger scale, the New York Stock Exchange provides the same kind of market. The stocks and bonds of 1,100 corporations are displayed on its counters. Its trading floor is a meeting place for buyers and sellers. The Exchange provides the machinery which permits John Smith in Portland, Oregon, to sell a share in a Texas oil company to Jane Smith in Portland, Maine—to sell his share quickly, for the highest price offered. The Exchange reports the news of the transaction and sees that John gets his money and Jane her stock certificate.

John and Jane never meet face to face. They are represented by brokers, members of the Exchange who make their living by buying and selling securities for the Smiths and the Johnsons and the Thompsons and the Joneses in every state. For each purchase or sale a broker makes, he charges his customer a commission. A fraction of this commission goes to the Exchange to finance the market machinery. The remainder of Exchange expenses are met by membership dues and fees from the corporations whose securities are listed on the Big Board. Eleven million dollars is collected annually from these sources; more than ten million is spent to operate the super-market.

The central figure in this market place is the broker, the man who owns a *seat* on the Exchange. Today, owning a seat entitles him to the privilege of standing up for five and a half hours a day in a crowded, noisy room. But it is a privilege so valuable that men paid more than half a million dollars for it in the boom days of 1929. And, it must be added, as little as $17,000 in 1942. Seat prices now range from $35,000 to $90,000, plus an initiation fee of $4,000 and dues of $750 a year.

The number of seats is limited, and it takes more than cash to buy one. An applicant for membership must prove that he is honest and financially responsible and even that his health is good. And he must be a man. All 1,366 members vehemently deny the existence of a rule against feminine seat owners, but the for-men-only tradition is so strong that no woman has yet been accepted for membership.

Each year, on the second Monday in May, four election booths are set up on the trading floor. Behind canvas curtains, members mark their ballots to elect a Board of Governors and its chairman. The Governors, who serve for three years, have final say on all policy matters connected with the operation of the super-market. They study membership applications and

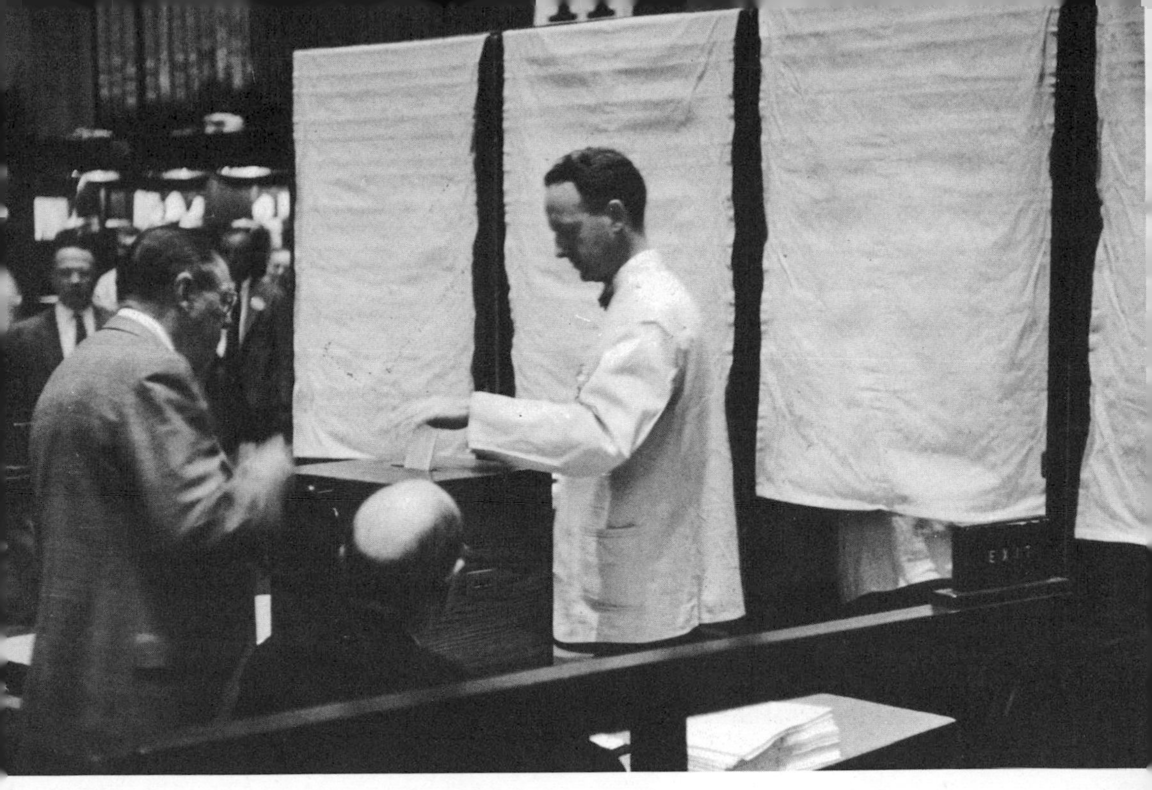

Stock Exchange Election Booths

discipline brokers who have disobeyed Exchange rules. They pass on budgets and decide which stocks and bonds should be listed for trading.

There are thirty-three Governors, twenty-nine of whom are elected by Exchange members. A president is appointed by the Board as executive head of the Exchange. He is the manager of the super-market, paid $100,000 a year to keep the sales machinery running smoothly. He appoints the remaining three members of the Board. They are known as the *public representatives,* because they have no direct connection with the securities business. Presently, two of them are corporation executives and the third a college president.

The Governors meet weekly in a handsome, high-ceilinged room lined with portraits of former Exchange presidents. The gilt-trimmed columns and niches are freshly painted, and a glowing red carpet was recently installed. Otherwise the room looks just as it did when it was completed in 1903.

Board of Governors' Meeting

The chairman of the Board presides, with a secretary at his side and the president facing him from the first row of seats. A gold name plate attached to each leather chair gives the name of the Governor to whom it is assigned. Some governors travel from as far as California and Washington, receiving a token payment of $20 for each meeting they attend.

The policies decided on by the Board are carried out by the president, with the help of the Exchange's 1,100 employees. The staff is responsible for all of the operations of the Big Board, from the physical comfort of members to the state of their account books.

Take a look at the crews of plumbers and electricians, engineers and carpenters who work in a maze of basements, four floors below street level. Over an ancient-looking forge, a machinist heats a metal bar to bend it into a hook. The machine shop repairs and makes new parts for the buildings' 700 motors.

Nearby is the electrical shop, stocked with lamps and fuses, and the plumbing shop, where all sheet-metal work is

Machine Shop

Carpenters' Shop

done. In the carpenters' room, doors are fitted, desks rebuilt, and shelves and cabinets made.

Largest of the basement areas is given over to air conditioning. One of the first U.S. businesses to control summer temperatures, the Exchange has had its own cooling system for fifty years. The machines you see in the picture on this page are 400-horsepower compressors, producing refrigeration to keep the trading floor at a year-round temperature in the seventies.

Despite these big compressors, the engineers face one problem that they have never been able to solve. When stock prices suddenly rise or fall and brokers are swamped with orders, the basement telephones jangle. Each call brings a complaint about the heat. "No thermostat will stand up against a busy market," an engineer explains. "All we can use then is psychology."

Next door to air cooling is air blowing. Pneumatic tubes are a basic part of the Exchange's internal network of com-

Air-Conditioning Machinery

Air-Blowing Machinery

munications. There are thirty-five miles of aluminum tubing underneath the trading floor, and shiny red cartridges stuffed with messages whiz from one part of the buildings to another all day long. The air pressure that pushes these carriers around is developed in the blower room, where a row of motors delivers 18,000 cubic feet of air each minute.

Above the basements there is a small but well-staffed hospital, an employees' cafeteria, and a private luncheon club for executive dining. In a dimly lit eighth floor room is a tailor shop, where guards and pages, elevator operators and messengers are fitted for 2,000 uniforms a year.

Central Records contains the files of all Exchange departments and a new microfilm machine to record important documents. The Mailing Division daily processes huge quantities of announcements and circulars. Its two offset presses print letters to members, quarterly reports, and confidential information.

In the Department of Research and Statistics is a library

Tailor Shop

Mailing Division

Library

of financial reference books, corporation balance sheets, and back files of newspapers. Economists, students, and the general public, as well as Exchange members, make use of the extensive collection of books and reports.

Two behind-the-scenes divisions directly responsible for the orderly operation of the super-market are the Department of Member Firms and the Department of Stock List. A majority of Exchange members are partners in brokerage companies that do business with the public, accepting customers' orders to buy and sell securities. These are *member firms,* companies in which at least one man owns a seat on the Exchange.

Before these firms may print the words "Members, New York Stock Exchange" on their office doors or in their advertisments, their financial standing and business methods are thoroughly investigated—and are subject to constant review. The Department of Member Firms orders surprise audits of account books and oversees the conduct of employees as well as partners. The men and women who deal directly with the public in handling buy and sell orders must pass a stiff examination before sitting down at their desks. Formerly called *customers' men,* they are now *registered representatives* who agree to abide by all Exchange rulings.

In somewhat the same way, the Department of Stock List polices the corporations whose securities are traded on the Exchange. It does not tell these companies how to run their businesses, but it sets up standards which must be met.

Before a corporation's stocks and bonds are accepted for listing on the super-market, its executives are asked to prove that they have a well-established business in which people from all parts of the country will be interested in investing. They must show $1,000,000 in earnings for the past year, at least 1,500 stockholders and 300,000 shares of outstanding stock. Their product must be well known, their future prospects good, and they must agree to the publication of quarterly financial reports.

Each year approximately 100 companies ask about listing

on the Exchange. After informal discussions with members of the Department of Stock List, the corporation submits a lengthy written application. This is studied carefully at a weekly meeting of the department, held in the committee room adjoining the Board of Governors' room. If the corporation meets Exchange requirements, its application is then forwarded to the Governors for a final decision.

Out of the hundred applicants, there are seldom more then twenty admitted for trading. In many instances the smaller corporations who are unable to meet Big Board standards are listed on the American Stock Exchange and the eighteen regional exchanges spotted across the country, in Philadelphia and Boston, in Chicago and Detroit, in St. Louis and Los Angeles. Brand-new companies just starting in business do not apply to the exchanges when they need capital. They go directly to the investment banker and underwriter, and their shares are sold in the over-the-counter securities market which you will read about in Chapter 9.

The Department of Stock List's work is not finished when a security is accepted. Corporations agree to notify the Exchange of all changes in their business, in their accounting methods, and the number of shares outstanding. Files are kept up to date, and in the department storeroom thousands of listing applications and company reports overflow the shelves

Company Reports in the Storeroom

Meeting of the Department of Stock List

and are stacked in piles on the floor. Studying these statements is a year-round job.

When a stock has passed its final examinations, it is introduced to the super-market with a flourish. Corporation executives, with visitors' badges pinned to their breast pockets, tour the trading floor to meet the men who will specialize in their shares. A photographer from the Department of Public Relations asks for a smile; a network of teletypes flashes a report to member-firm offices and newspapers. New merchandise is on display and buyers must be informed that it is available!

CHAPTER 4 100 shares of Amalgamated Baseball Bat change hands

The heart of the Exchange is the trading floor, a room five stories high, almost as big as a football field. Polished wood floors, marble block walls, tall narrow windows through which Wall Street's dust-filtered sun trickles in. Let's take a look at it some weekday morning at nine. From the Visitors Gallery on the north wall, the big room is orderly and quiet. Its few occupants walk slowly and their whispers echo in the emptiness.

Gradually the sounds increase. There's a murmur of voices as clerks mill around, sharpening pencils, finding their places beside telephones or inside the horseshoe-shaped booths. Brokers stroll in more leisurely, unzipping brief cases, studying the notes on their memo pads.

The sounds grow louder. Machinery noises. The clackety-clack of tickers, the snap of pneumatic tubes being tested. Directly below you, a man with a screw driver repairs a projector. Voices are louder, too, and there's a tap-tap-tap that's hard to place. It turns out to be the sound of men drumming on the counters with their fingernails as they wait for the beginning of the trading day!

At nine fifty-eight an Exchange employee appears on the pulpit-like balcony projecting from the east wall. There's a microphone in front of him and the balcony is flanked by loud-speakers. At nine fifty-nine and forty-five seconds, he rises. Precisely at ten the gong beside him rings. There are no announcements to make today. The important thing is that the gong has rung and the market is open for trading.

Immediately, the pace quickens. The murmur of voices rises to a roar. Men scurry back and forth, shouting, waving their hands, tearing up scraps of paper, and tossing them into the air. Occasionally a cheer or boo is heard. Phones buzz.

A new stock is listed for trading

The Trading Floor at 9 A.M.

Tickers whir. Below you, the projectors flash the news of sales onto narrow screens across the floor. Two big blackboards that you took to be wall decorations have come alive. Parts of them flap up like shutters, revealing white numbers underneath. It's as if the room and its occupants were in a movie being shown at fast speed. Confusion, noise, litter, where all was peace a few minutes earlier.

You try to understand what's going on, but there are a hundred things, a thousand things happening at once, and you can't sort them out or keep track of them. Instead of trying to watch all parts of the floor at the same time, let's follow one transaction.

Pretend first that you're at home with some extra money that you'd like to invest. You've been looking into the stock of Amalgamated Baseball Bat and you're convinced that it is a sound investment that will pay you dividends. Perhaps you've talked it over with your broker too. At any rate, you

The Trading Floor at 10:05

pick up the phone and call him. He may be a partner in a member firm or one of the firm's registered representatives. After asking him for the current price of Amalgamated Baseball Bat, you announce:

"I want to buy 100 shares."

"At the market?" he asks.

"At the market," you agree.

At the market means that you will take the stock at the best price your broker can buy it for you at the time he receives your order. This "best" price is the lowest if you are buying stock, the highest if you are selling.

After the man you have been talking to receives your order, it is telephoned to the floor of the Exchange. Hurry back to the Visitors' Gallery now so that you can see what happens.

Lining the room are open telephone booths, ten phones to a booth, 1,160 telephones altogether. These telephones are

The gong rings at 10

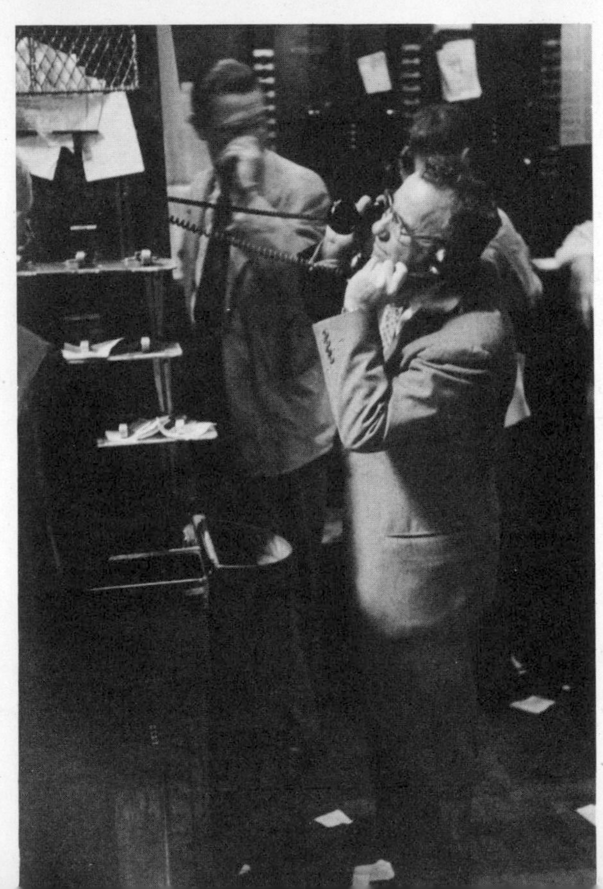

Telephone Clerks

Repairing a Projector

Annunciator Board

direct wires, connecting member-firm offices with the trading floor. A firm may rent one or twenty-five, depending on the volume of its business. The telephone clerks are member-firm employees who must remain within the area of the booths. In years gone by a brass strip set in the floor marked their boundaries. Now there is only an imaginary line that the clerks are forbidden to cross.

Watch the man who receives your order. It's a busy day and he's trying to talk into two telephones at once. He writes out the messages on one of several pads in front of him. Yours goes on a slip of white paper with BUY printed on it. If you were selling, it would go on a SELL form. Cancellations of orders are written on yellow pads, requests for information on pink or blue.

The message is short. "100 BAT." Why "BAT"? Time and space are at a premium on the Exchange, and every stock has an official abbreviation and often a semi-official nickname. United States Steel is written as "X" and Pepsi-Cola as "PEP."

1,160 Telephones

Broker's Badge

BUY

100

BAT

mkt

SHEARSON, HAMMILL & CO.

________________X

Buy Order

If you want to sound like a Wall Streeter be sure to refer to Bethlehem Steel as "Bessie," the Missouri-Kansas-Texas Railroad as "Katie," and Montgomery Ward as "Monkey."

As he writes, the clerk presses a button connected to the black boards you've been wondering about. These are *annunciator boards,* used to signal the brokers on the floor, where it's far too noisy for buzzers or bells to be heard. The clerk's push button causes one of the flaps on the board to drop so that the number behind it is visible. Every member of the Exchange has his own number. When he sees it on the board he knows that his clerk is paging him.

Mr. Jones, the floor partner of your member firm, shoulders his way through the crowds. He walks quickly, but he never runs, because he can be fined for running, just as he can be fined for smoking on the floor or wearing a stiff-brimmed hat. He is the man who does the actual buying and selling, the man who own the seat. He is known as a *commission broker* because he charges a commission for filling your order. Along with everyone else on the trading floor, he wears

"Squad!"

a badge giving his name, his firm name, and his annunciator-board number. His badge is white. Other floor badges are two-colored, red, yellow, or green.

Taking the message from the clerk's outstretched hand, Jones reads it as he heads for one of the horseshoe-shaped booths. Not to any one of the eighteen booths, but to the only one at which shares of Amalgamated Baseball Bat may be bought and sold. These booths are *trading posts,* and each listed stock is permanently assigned to one of them. Shares of Hershey's chocolate are traded at Post 15, Canada Dry Ginger Ale at 3, Quaker Oats at 7, National Biscuit Company at 11. Inactive stocks in which there is little daily trading are grouped together at Post 30.

By now you probably have some questions. Are the horseshoe-shaped counters called trading posts because the name goes back to Indian days? Why "Post 30" when the other posts are numbered from 1 to 18? The answers to your questions could well be "just because." Just because things have always been that way.

Bidding for Stock

The Crowd at a Trading Post

The Stock Exchange's trading posts do not date back to colonial times. The name originated in 1894, when actual wooden posts were installed on the floor to mark the place where a specific stock could be traded. The U-shaped counters have been in use for more than twenty-five years, but they are still "posts." Similarly, Post 30 was numbered when there were thirty posts instead of nineteen. The old names stick. Just as the New York Stock Exchange is still "the Big Board" and the American Stock Exchange "the Curb."

Mr. Jones joins a group of men standing at one side of the trading post.

"How's BAT?" he shouts.

"Twelve and a half to three quarters," one of the men answers.

"I'll give five eighths for 100," Jones calls out.

"Sold," another broker replies.

The two men step aside. They jot down each other's name and the price they have agreed on. No money changes hands, nor is there any written contract. But you are now the owner of 100 shares of Amalgated Baseball Bat.

Mr. Jones waves the slip of paper on which he has noted the transaction. He shouts "Squad!" until a uniformed page takes it from him and delivers it to his clerk. The details of the purchase are telephoned to the member-firm office and will soon be reported to you. The whole transaction has taken less time than you would spend biking to the corner grocery store for a quart of milk.

But what happened? Your broker didn't join just any group of men around the trading post. He entered *the crowd* interested in buying and selling shares of Amalgamated Baseball Bat. If you had wanted to buy U.S. Steel shares, he would have joined the *steel crowd;* if General Motors, the *motors crowd.*

When he asked, "How's BAT?" he was saying, "At what prices are people willing to buy and sell Amalgamated Baseball Bat now?" The answer he received, "Twelve and a half to

Brokers exchange names after a sale

three quarters," meant that the highest bid to buy BAT, at that moment, was $12.50 a share, and the lowest offer to sell was $12.75.

He could have bought the stock imediately for $12.75, but he wanted to buy at the lowest possible price. Therefore, he offered to "give five eighths," to buy the stock for 12⅝s or $12.62½ a share. Another member of the crowd whose customer wanted to sell 100 shares of BAT accepted the offer.

Perhaps you've been to an auction where the auctioneer holds up an article and asks, "How much am I bid?" Everyone interested in buying calls out a price and the article goes to the highest bidder. The buyers compete, but there is only one seller. The Stock Exchange operates a *two-way auction,* with buyers competing to get the lowest price and sellers competing for the highest. When two brokers, one representing a buyer and one a seller, agree on a price, a sale is made.

All bids and offers must be made in a loud voice so that anyone interested can join in. Suppose someone else wanted to buy BAT and his broker shouted, "I'll give five eighths" at the same moment Mr. Jones did. Who then would be the purchaser? The question is quickly decided by having the competing brokers match coins. The winner takes the stock; the loser goes back to the crowd to bid again.

On a day in which there is a great deal of activity in a particular stock, there may be four or five brokers matching. From the balcony, you can see the coins flashing in the air. The picture on page 61 shows a tense, excited crowd, with brokers elbowing their way in to listen to the trading, and shouting themselves hoarse to make themselves heard.

All over the floor men pause to watch the busy group. If the stock's price moves quickly upward, the spectators respond with cheers or earsplitting whistles. If it goes down, there are boos. Torn-up bits of paper float through the air as brokers gesture nervously or engage in a bit of horseplay to relieve tense feelings.

There are quiet days, too, when members lean against

Torn-up bits of paper float through the air

Matching Coins

Trying a New Golf Club

the posts discussing the Dodgers' chances or unlimber their muscles by trying out a new golf club. During such a lull they sometimes drift to the lounge adjoining the floor to play bridge or backgammon and puff at a cigar. But these periods of calm seldom last long. As soon as an order is telephoned in, games are interrupted, cigars put aside. Brass racks on the wall at the entrance to the trading floor are filled with unfinished smokes at the end of the day.

By three o'clock you can sympathize with the broker below you who is giving his weary feet a few minutes' rest as he sits on one of the little jump seats outside a trading post—the only seat to which his membership on the Exchange entitles him. He's more interested now in talking about foot powders and corn plasters than he is in discussing the activities of the market.

At three twenty-nine there's a brief flurry of activity as brokers hasten to fill last-minute orders. Then the gong rings, a fifteen-second announcement that all trading must cease until 10 A.M. tomorow. Clerks and members pick up their note pads and hats, close their brief cases, and glance at the report of final sales.

By three-forty the flag that flies outside the window over Wall Street has been hauled in. Inside, the big room is empty, its floor bright with bits of colored paper, as if it had been sprinkled with confetti. A staff of clean-up men take over. With their broad brooms they slowly push the day's debris into great piles in the center of the room.

The Trading Floor at 3:45

Inside the Trading Post

Tube Man

Odd-Lot Order

BUY

10

BAT

mkt.

~~CANCEL~~

@

560 - SHEARSON, HAMMILL & CO.

______________ NO. ____________ X-11

CHAPTER 5 Two thousand people

There are nearly 2,000 people on the trading floor of the New York Stock Exchange. You've watched several of them in action in the simplest of stock market transactions. To meet some of the others, suppose you now decide to buy only 10 shares of Amalgamated Baseball Bat.

When the telephone clerk receives this order he does not put up Jones's number on the annunciator board. Instead he stuffs the order slip into a red wooden cartridge, known as a *widget,* and sends it by pneumatic tube to the post where BAT is traded. It is received there by the *tube man* stationed inside the post. After stamping the exact time on the order, the tube man slips it into a little wooden tree at the end of his counter. The *odd-lot dealer* picks it up from there.

Since Civil War days the standard trading unit has been 100 shares of stock or some multiple of 100 (200, 300, 500)—a *round lot.* However, it has always been possible to buy 1 share or 17 shares or 99 shares of any listed stock. This is an *odd-lot order* and two Exchange member firms specialize in filling them.

The 10 shares of stock that you have ordered will not be bought from a customer who wants to sell. Instead, they will come from the odd-lot dealer's own supply. The price at which he sells to you is determined by the price of the first round-lot sale taking place after he receives your order. If BAT sells for 12⅝ this morning, the odd-lot dealer will sell to you for $12.75 a share, charging you an eighth of a point for his services. Although you are buying stock owned by his firm, the amount you pay for it is regulated by the auction market.

When the odd-lot dealer picks up your order, he makes a note of it in the pocket-sized alphabetical file which he carries. As soon as there has been a round-lot sale of BAT, he fills out a sales report on your purchase. His report is placed in the brass cup at the base of the wooden tree that you see in the picture on this page. After a clerk time-stamps it, it is sent back by pneumatic tube to your own broker's telephone booth. The time stamp and the Exchange's report of round-lot transactions permit you to check on the fairness of the price you have paid.

Roughly a third of all orders are for odd lots. Because of this large volume of business, the odd-lot firms employ other Exchange members to work for them, in return for a commission on each transaction. These men are *associate brokers* or *floor brokers.*

In addition to the floor broker who fills odd-lot orders, there is also the *two-dollar broker.* He is a member of the

Odd-Lot Tree

Odd-Lot Dealer's File

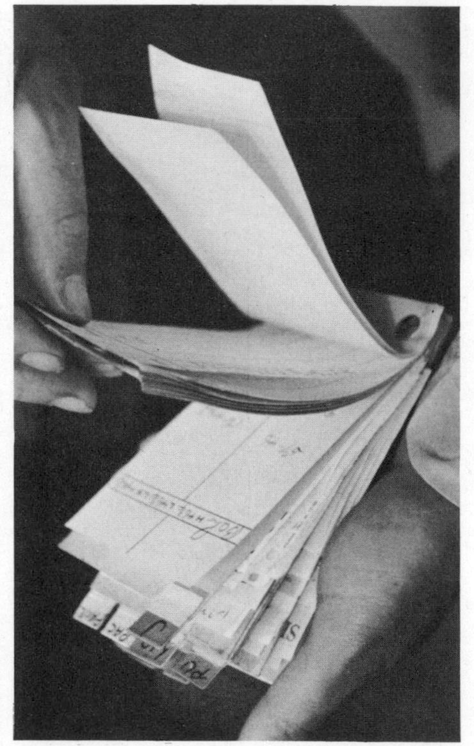

BUY ______________195___

100
BAT 11½

G. T. C.

BUY

100
BAT 11½

SHEARSON, HAMMILL & CO.

______________________X

KINDLY SIGN ATTACHED RECEIPT AND SEND TO

W. E. HUTTON & CO.

Y-2

Limit Orders

Exchange who buys and sells for Mr. Jones and other commission brokers when they are busy. Years ago he was paid $2.00 for each 100-share purchase or sale. Today a more appropriate name for him would be *three-dollar broker.*

There are still other kinds of orders that you can place. Perhaps you think the price of BAT is going to drop. Instead of buying at the market you can tell Jones not to buy for you until the stock has gone down to 11½ or lower. This is a *limit order,* and it may be placed for one day only or *G.T.C.*—good till canceled.

The telephone clerk's slip for a limit order will look like the two reproduced on this page. When Jones receives it, he has to decide whether or not he has time to stand at the BAT trading post until the stock drops to 11½. Usually he's too busy, so he turns your order over to the BAT *specialist.*

A specialist is a member who trades exclusively in one or more particular stocks. Like the odd-lot dealers and two-dollar brokers, he never works directly for the public. He acts as an agent for other brokers and is paid a commission by them.

Your order is immediately entered in his *book,* a black loose-leaf notebook with space for buy orders on the left-hand page and sell orders on the right. When BAT sells for 11½ and the specialist buys it for you, he notifies Mr. Jones. Your G.T.C. order is good for three months. It must be renewed then or it is automatically canceled.

The specialist also buys and sells for his own account, to maintain an orderly market in his stock. Suppose, for instance, that the bids to buy BAT ranged from $11 to $12, while the lowest offer to sell was $13. The specialist would step in with a compromise, offering to buy perhaps at $12.25 or to sell at $12.75. Similarly, if the price of his stock was moving up rapidly, he would be expected to sell his own shares for less than the public was offering.

Exchange traditions trace the origin of the specialist back to 1875, when a member named Boyd broke his leg. Unable to move around the floor, he hobbled to a seat in the middle of the crowd trading in Western Union stock and filled orders only in these shares. By the time his leg had mended, he found that he was making more money as a specialist in Western Union shares than he had before. Other specialists soon followed Mr. Boyd, until today one out of every four Exchange members maintains a permanent station at one of the trading posts.

At the opposite extreme from the specialist is the *floor trader,* a member who buys and sells only for himself. He travels from post to post in search of quick profits. He may buy BAT in the morning for 12½ and sell it in the afternoon for 12¾. A transaction of this kind which is completed in one day is called *daylight trading.* Nowadays the floor trader's activities are restricted by Exchange and government rules, as well as by high income taxes. In 1933 there were eighty-six floor traders. Today there are only twenty.

Most of the people inside the trading post are clerks who work for specialists. Outside, at the edge of the crowd, stands the *reporter,* an Exchange employee who records all trans-

A Specialist

actions in the stocks to which he is assigned. One of his jobs is to keep the *last-sale indicators* up to date. Mounted on the outer wall of the post, these indicators show the last price of each of the post's stocks. In the picture on page 76 a reporter is changing the price of Universal Pictures (UVL).

Even before he sets the price indicator, the reporter hands a record of the sale to a nearby *carrier page*. From a tube station at one end of the horseshoe, this record is sent by pneumatic tube to the Ticker Room, so that it can be teletyped across the country, as you will see in Chapter 6. The reporter, who usually covers a quarter of the stocks at each trading post, wears a black jacket, the page a gray one with the letter C—for carrier—on his sleeve.

At the opposite end of the horseshoe from the carrier page, you'll find the *quotation clerk*. He wears earphones and a mouthpiece clamped to his head. Whenever a broker makes a new bid to buy or an offer to sell, the quote clerk telephones

Last-Sale Indicator

Quotation Clerk

Carrier Page

the change to the Quotation Room. From there the information becomes available to you, and to John Smith in Oregon and Jane Smith in Maine, through the member firms which represent you.

Not far from the stock trading floor is the Bond Room. The *bond crowd* also assembles each morning at ten. When a broker has a request to buy, he steps into *the ring* and in a loud voice calls out his bid. The ring is a space, roughly four by six feet, outlined on the floor by a strip of brass. The broker representing a buyer is joined in the ring by sellers. Bidding continues until a price is agreed on. Then the buyer shouts, "Take them!" or the seller, "Sold!" A reporter stationed beside the brokers keeps a record of the sales for the bond ticker.

Often the broker with a buy order cannot immediately locate a seller. When this happens, he places his order in a metal file cabinet known as a *can.* Suppose a broker is asked to buy five bonds of the Dinkeytown Railroad. The *can clerk* writes out his bid on a card and places it in the Dinkeytown file. Days later, another broker receives an order to sell Dinkeytown bonds. He takes the bid card from the can and steps into the ring. Loudly he announces his offer to sell. The buyer's broker joins him, and if there are no competing bids the two men dicker until they agree on a price.

In recent years there has been a decline in the number of bonds traded on the Exchange, with a large part of the nation's bond business—particularly government bonds—moving to the over-the-counter market. Although any Exchange member may act as either bond or stockbroker, there are now only eighteen men who devote their business day exclusively to bonds.

Travel now from the quiet of the Bond Room to the tumultuous trading floor of the American Stock Exchange a few blocks away. The structure of the Curb closely resembles that of the Big Board. Its 499 members are brokers, most of them engaged in buying and selling securities for the public. Curb seats sell for $10,000 to $21,000, with an all-time high of

Bond Crowd in the Ring

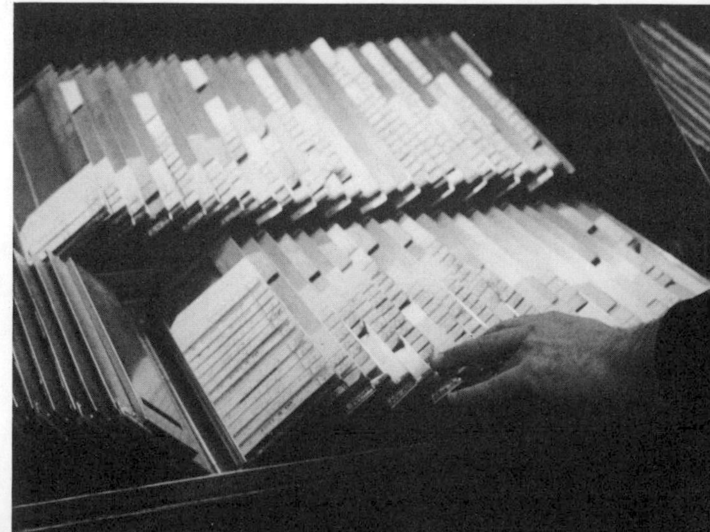

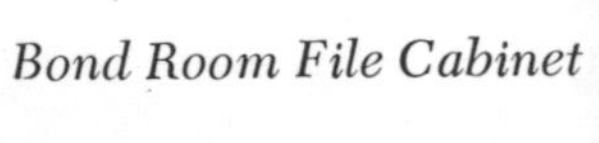

Bond Room File Cabinet

Telephone Clerks on the American Stock Exchange

$254,000 in 1929 and a low of $650 in 1942. Most large brokerage houses own seats on both the New York and American Stock Exchanges.

The corporations whose stocks are listed on the Curb are, on the whole, smaller than those traded on the Big Board, but they are required to be soundly financed companies with likely future prospects. Many of the securities have names that you will recognize from their products: Spalding baseballs, Fairchild airplane engines, Hormel ham, Singer sewing machines, Benrus watches, Kaiser cars. The Curb is also the largest market for foreign securities in the United States.

On a trading floor slightly smaller than the New York Stock Exchange's, the Curb operates a two-way auction market which is just as efficient and perhaps a little faster-moving than the Big Board's. The Curb's claim for a speed record is based on the hand signals inherited from street-market days.

Along two sides of the floor there are tiers of seats resembling the grandstand at a football game. Members' clerks sit here, facing the brokers. They are connected by private telephone wires to member-firm offices and receive all orders to buy and sell. As soon as an order comes in, the clerk rises and hastens to attract his boss's attention. He does this by shouting "Yoo hoo" or "Hallo-o," by clapping his hands, by whistling—by any previously agreed-on sound. No matter where he is on the floor, the broker recognizes his clerk's signal and turns his head. The clerk then proceeds to pass along the order through sign language.

Clerks and brokers have worked out a complete alphabet and number system. A raised fist with the thumb sticking out represents "A." For "B," the fist is opened and the fingers lightly pressed together. "C" is an open hand, with the forefinger and thumb outlining the letter. "One" and "100" are signaled by a pointing forefinger. For "10," the index finger points down; for "50," the thumb jerks up.

An entire word or phrase can also be communicated by a single gesture. The palm of the hand facing upward means "Buy"; the palm downward, "Sell." "Yes" is signaled with the thumb, the index finger, and little finger. If the clerk wants to ask about the size of the market, he holds out both hands as fond parents do when they say, "How big is Baby? So-o-o big."

As soon as the broker has bought the stock, he turns again toward his clerk. "Complete," he signals by a quick salute. "Bought at 25½." If there has been a delay, he can report on that too. When he points his forefinger at his head, he is saying, "Ahead . . . an order is ahead of mine."

On a slow trading day, brokers and clerks amuse themselves by eavesdropping on each other's conversations. Do you see that clerk in the middle of the grandstand? He's opening and closing his hand rapidly, raising one finger after another in great excitement. There must be a big financial deal under way.

"No." The broker who is showing you around shakes his head. "He's just telling a friend of his on the floor to meet him at the cafeteria around the corner at 12 sharp."

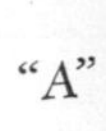

"A"

"B"

"C"

"Yes"

"How big is the market?"

"Ahead . . . an order is ahead of mine"

CHAPTER 6 Time means money

Back in Andrew Jackson's day there were few investors who lived outside New York or the major cities along the East Coast. If you were a Chicagoan wishing to buy stocks or bonds you would probably travel to New York to make your purchase. Otherwise weeks might elapse between the time you wrote to your broker to ask for current prices and he received your order to buy or sell. Weeks in which the stock in which you were interested might have doubled in price or dropped to a disastrous low. Suppose Erie Canal was selling for $30 when your broker read your inquiry, for $35 when you received his answer, for $40 when your order finally reached him. One hundred shares of stock would cost you $1,000 more than you anticipated!

Time means money in the stock market, and time must be measured not only in weeks and days but in minutes and seconds. Before the Exchange could become a national market place it had to find ways for speedy communication. Investors in New York were informed of changes in stock prices by a crew of messengers known as *pad-shovers.* All during trading hours these young men collected figures from the Exchange and then ran from one brokerage office to another, shouting out the latest prices.

A more elaborate system was worked out to send messages to Philadelphia financiers. While mail was still traveling by stagecoach, the New York Stock & Exchange Board manned a series of stations on hills and ridges across the state of New Jersey. Each station was equipped with semaphore signals for sending messages and telescopes as an aid in receiving them. Information about stock prices could be wigwagged in as short a time as ten minutes from New York to Philadelphia. The telegraph put the semaphore out of business in 1844, but it was

Ticker Room

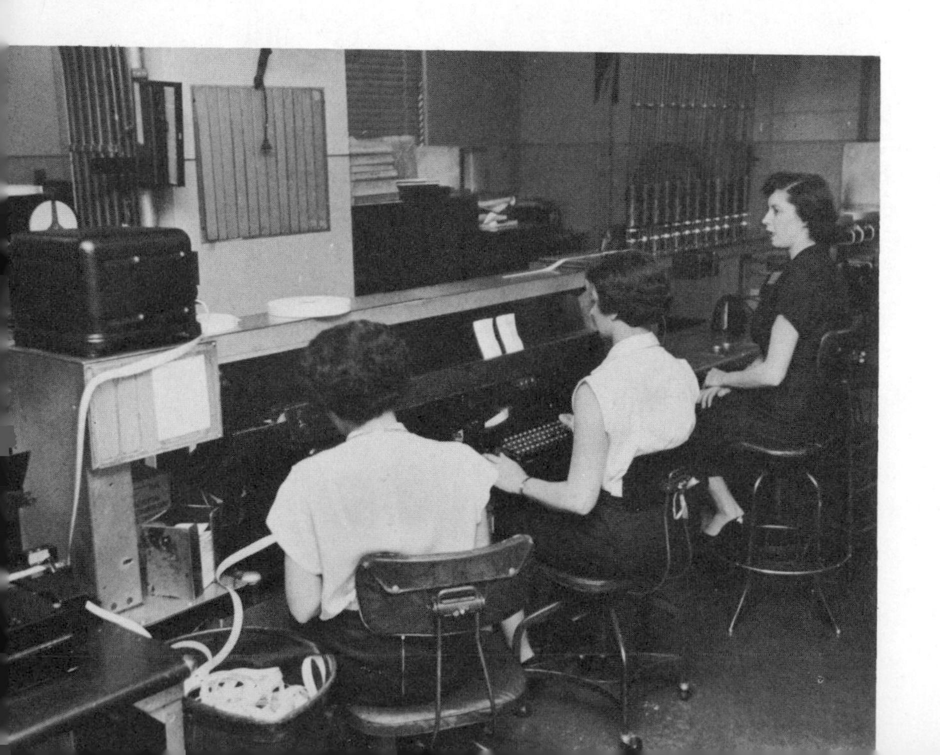

not until after the Civil War that pad-shovers were replaced by stock tickers.

The stock ticker is a high-speed printing telegraph that records all sales on a narrow strip of tape. As soon as Mr. Jones concluded your purchase of 100 shares of Amalgamated Baseball Bat, a report of the transaction traveled to a busy room on the Exchange's fifth floor. The picture on page 84 shows the pneumatic-tube terminals in the Ticker Room where it was received. The widget containing the information about your purchase drops through the wire cage to the counter in front of a clerk. She removes the slip of paper which the carrier page had placed there a moment before. From her hands it travels along a moving belt to the ticker operators.

Seated in front of a machine that looks like a typewriter, the ticker operator reports your purchase on a roll of narrow paper tape. Her machine punches holes in the tape rather than printing letters. These perforations are translated into electrical impulses and sent across the country by a battery of vacuum tubes. At the same moment, tickers in Los Angeles and Boston and New Orleans print the fact that someone has bought 100 shares of Amalgamated Baseball Bat at 12⅝.

The details of your transaction are reported on 2,232 tickers in 384 cities in 46 states, and in Canada and Cuba as well. On the busiest day in the history of the Exchange—October 29, 1929—5,000 miles of tape unrolled from the tickers. Today the daily figure would be closer to 400 miles.

See if you can read a piece of the tape. The letters at the top give the names of the stocks. AC stands for American Can Company, T for American Telephone & Telegraph, C for Chrysler Corporation, KT for Missouri-Kansas-Texas Rail-

Ticker Tape

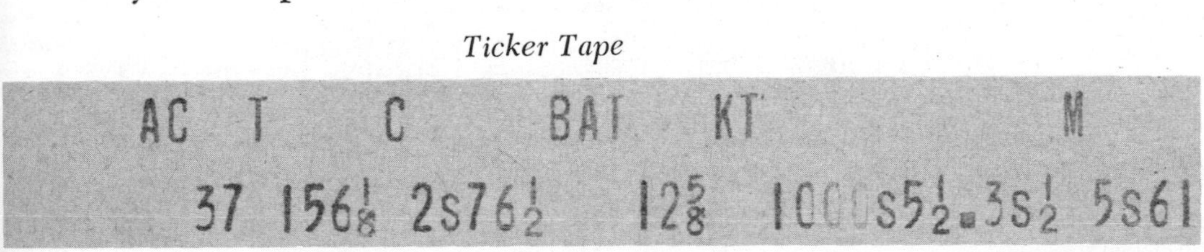

AC T C BAT KT M

37 156⅛ 2S76½ 12⅝ 1000S5½.3S½ 5S61

road, M for Montgomery Ward. BAT you recognize, of course, as your own purchase of Amalgamated Baseball Bat.

If only 100 shares of stock are sold, the price alone is printed. One hundred shares of American Can were traded for $37 a share, 100 shares of American Tel & Tel for $156.12½ a share, 100 shares of Amalgamated Baseball Bat for $12.62½.

The "2s" under Chrysler means that 200 shares were traded. The "5s" under Monkey represents 500 shares. One thousand shares of Katie went for $5.50, followed immediately by 300 shares at the same price. Notice that in the second transaction "5" was not repeated and only the fraction appeared on the tape.

The ticker can print 500 characters a minute, but there are often times when this is not fast enough to keep up with the activity on the trading floor. Then the tape is spoken of as being *late* and even more abbreviations are used. Instead of writing out the selling price of BAT at 12⅝, the ticker shortens it to 2⅝. The price of American Can is listed as 7, American Tel & Tel as 6⅛, Chrysler as 6½, and so forth. Anyone following the tape closely would know that these stocks were selling in the 10s, the 30s, or the 150s. All he needs is the report of the final digit and fraction to keep up to the minute.

The stock ticker with its continuously moving tape has limitations. It can be read conveniently only by a few people at a time. To overcome this problem, exchange and brokerage houses project the tape on illuminated screens, in the same way that motion pictures are projected. There are five of these screens (called *Trans-Luxes,* after the name of the manufacturer of the projection system) on the main trading floor of the New York Stock Exchange, one reporting bond sales and four, stocks.

No matter where a broker is standing, he can always follow the last sales as they are flashed on the Trans-Lux. The screen in the picture on page 88 tells him that 500 shares of Seaboard Finance Company (SFC) have sold for $23.50, that 100 shares of National Lead Company (LT) have sold for

Vacuum tubes send news of stock sales

Reading the Ticker

Trans-Lux Screen

$32.50, 100 shares of Melville Shoe Corporation (MES) for $27, and 400 shares of York Corporation (YOK) for $22.12½.

Members of the New York Stock Exchange learn about trading on the Curb through a ticker stationed at the entrance of the trading floor. The Curb, however, uses Trans-Lux screens to report its own transactions, those of the Big Board, and the sales of stocks on the Toronto Stock Exchange.

Before you placed your order for Amalgamated Baseball Bat, your broker gave you not only the latest sales price as reported on the ticker, but also the current *quotation* on the stock. A quotation, on Wall Street, does not mean a paragraph from the Gettysburg Address or some lines from Shakespeare. It means reporting the highest bid to buy a stock and the lowest offer to sell. The quotation on BAT just before you bought it was 12½ bid, 12¾ offered. It could be learned by entering the BAT crowd on the trading floor. It could also be learned by telephoning any member-firm office.

When you ask your broker for "the quote on BAT," he turns to a private telephone set on his desk. Dialing 22, BAT's special code number, he is immediately connected with a clerk in the Exchange's Quotation Room. He need only say "BAT" to have her give the latest quotation. In a few seconds he can pass it along to you.

The rapid quotation system starts on the trading floor with the quotation clerk, whose picture you saw on page 76. His report of new bids and offers goes to *posting girls* in the Quotation Room. Directly above them are electrically operated blackboards with space for each listed stock. As soon as they receive new quotes from the floor, they change the figures on the boards.

The Quotation Room has two boards, so placed that telephone clerks in the center of the long narrow room can always read the figures. Your broker speaks to one of these clerks when he dials 22. She is responsible for quotations on fifty or so stocks with the same code number. As soon as he says "BAT," she looks at the panels facing her and answers, "12½ to ¾."

To make its quotation system even faster, the Exchange has recently installed automatic tape announcers for the 200 most active stocks. When your broker dials the code number for U. S. Steel or General Motors, he hears the quote immediately without having to ask for the stock by name. The automatic tapes, recorded on the trading floor, are similar to those used by telephone companies to announce the weather or the correct time.

The work load of the Quotation Department varies, depending on the amount of trading being done. On a busy day in 1937, 173,793 quotes were given out. Today the number of calls averages 65,500, a total of 16,500,000 quotations a year. The American Stock Exchange's quotation division answers more than 8,000,000 calls in a year.

Quotation Room

CHAPTER 7 More machinery

You became the owner of 100 shares of Amalgamated Baseball Bat the moment the word "Sold!" was shouted on the trading floor. The actual stock certificate will travel through many hands, however, before it reaches yours. If your purchase was made on Monday morning, the seller's broker must deliver the shares to Mr. Jones by Friday noon. He has four days in which to obtain the stock from his customer, who may live in Texas or Oregon. Meanwhile, you have a job to do too. You must pay for the stock—$1,262.50, plus a broker's commission of $17.63. There are federal and state transfer taxes also, but these are paid by the seller.

On Friday morning 100 shares of BAT are placed inside an ordinary-looking manila envelope. A messenger from the seller's member firm carries them to the Exchange's Broad Street building and tosses them into a slot mounted on the building's outer wall. The manila envelope slides down a chute resembling a mail chute and lands on a counter in a basement room. Your stock has now been delivered to the Stock Clearing Corporation.

Stock Clearing is operated by the Exchange to assist buyer and seller in completing their trade. Certificates brought here by the seller are delivered to the buyer. Each envelope carries a ticket listing the cash value of the securities inside and the member firm to whom it is addressed. Clerks in the basement room sort the envelopes into boxes similar to post-office boxes, one for each member firm.

Just before the noon deadline, securities slide down the chute faster than the clerks can distribute them. The pile of envelopes in the picture on page 92 contains stocks and bonds worth more than a million dollars.

Exactly at noon the chute is closed for the day and the

clerks hurriedly complete their sorting. A gong rings a minute later, the signal that the Distributing Department is open for business. Even while it is sounding, men crowd around the department's barred windows. These men are *runners,* messengers from member firms who have been sent to collect the securities in their firms' boxes.

Thirty years ago runners were eager youngsters starting out as messengers in the hope of someday owning an Exchange seat. Now they are more likely to be elderly men who stow the certificates in their brief cases slowly and walk out with an unhurried air. Armed guards check identification cards as they enter and leave, the only sign that the exchange of securities is not as casual as it seems.

The crowded corridor is empty by twelve-fifteen, but work is just beginning for Stock Clearing's bookkeepers. Mr. Jones's firm is receiving shares for some of his customers and

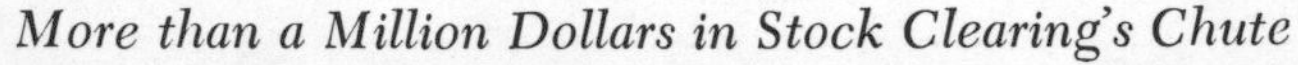

More than a Million Dollars in Stock Clearing's Chute

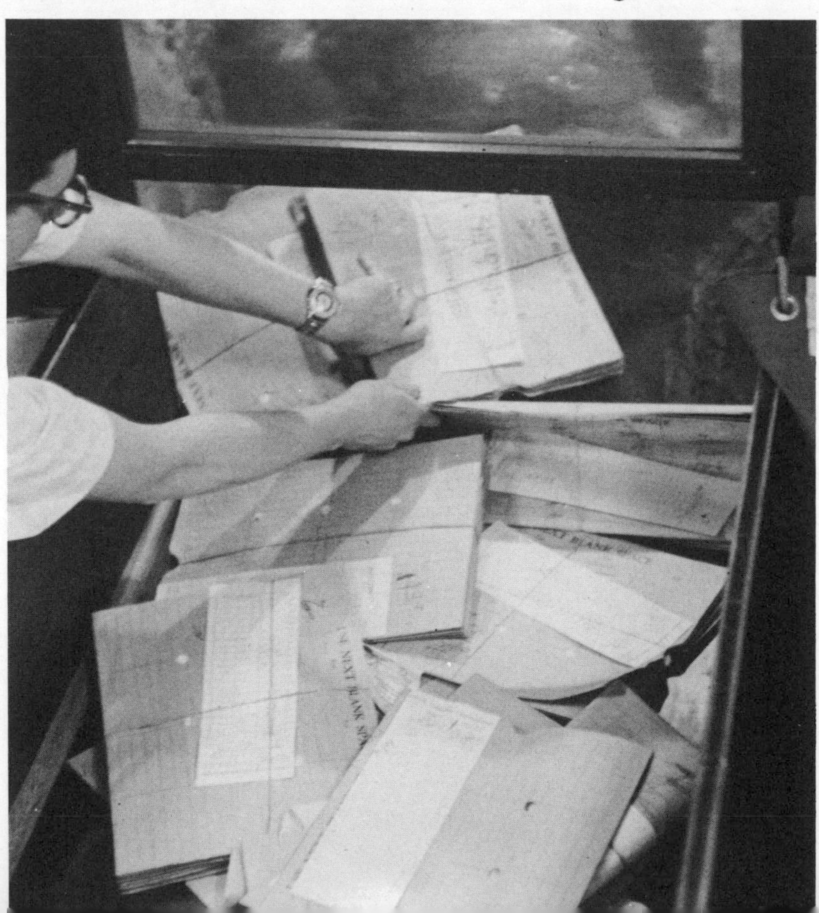

Distributing Department, Stock Clearing Corporation

delivering for others. Instead of paying or collecting separately for each transaction, he depends on Stock Clearing to keep accounts for him. Rows of tabulating machines in the Clearance Department are busy from noon until after dark compiling daily records of purchases and sales for the member firms.

While the accounting machines buzz away, a runner delivers yours shares of BAT to Jones's office. Your shares, but not yet your shares. The stock certificate still carries the name of the man who sold it to you. As far as the officers of Amalgamated Baseball Bat know, he is the owner and it is to him that they will send dividends and notices of stockholders' meetings. The final step in the transfer of the stock is to take it to an employee of the corporation, known as a *transfer agent*. Every company whose stock is listed on the Exchange must maintain a transfer agent in the Wall Street district. When a messenger

Clearance Department

brings the stock to him, he issues a new certificate with your name printed on it.

During the time that the messenger is at the transfer agent's, perhaps you'd like to visit your member firm. Some firms have only one office, located near the Exchange, and two or three employees. Others, known as *wire houses,* have thousands of employees and branch offices in every major U.S. city. The phrase *wire house* was first used in 1873 when a Wall Street firm installed a private telegraph line to its uptown office on Twenty-third Street. Today there are 500,000 miles of private telephone and telegraph wires linking member-firm offices. The largest of the wire houses has more than 4,000 employees, 114 branch offices, and more than 600 teletype machines.

Your firm is a middling-big one, with three dozen branches and four partners on the floor of the Exchange. You

Customers' Room in a Member Firm

Electric Stock Board

Order Room of Member Firm

Checking Stock Certificates

are made to feel at home in the Customers' Room, where you may ask for advice from a broker or registered representative or sit and study the course of the day's market. Small firms have stock tickers for their customers, but in many large offices the ticker has been replaced by Trans-Lux screens and electric *stock boards*.

These boards have separate panels for as many as 500 active stocks. Each panel lists yesterday's closing price, the price at the opening of today's market, the highest and lowest prices today, as well as the last sale. Whenever there is a shift in the price of any stock that is *boarded*, the figures change automatically. The boards are operated by the Teleregister Corporation, an affiliate of Western Union.

Next door to the Customers' Room is the Order Room. Here rows of teletype machines and telephones permit split-second communication with branch offices and with the trading floor of the Exchange. As you watch, the girl in the foreground of the picture on page 96 receives a message from Los Angeles to buy 200 shares of Beech-Nut at the market.

"It's a race!" she says as she hands the order slip to the clerk who sits facing her. "Race" means "quick" in Wall Street jargon. "Orders from the Coast are always marked 'race,'" the supervisor explains with a smile.

From here the order goes by private wire to the firm's telephone clerk at the Exchange. If the market in Beech-Nut is an active one, the transaction is completed in a matter of minutes. The clerk then hands a report of the purchase to the teletypist, and she sends a reply to Los Angeles: "Bought 200 Beech-Nut at 29¾." Less than five minutes have elapsed between the time the order was placed in Los Angeles and the report of its execution is received there.

By now the messenger has returned from the transfer agent and your stock is almost ready for delivery. It is waiting in the sorting pen, where the man you see in the picture on page 96 must check through all newly transferred securities to be sure that they have been made out correctly. Your certificate will be mailed to you before the end of the day, unless you have asked your broker to keep it for you.

Many member-firm customers leave their securities with their brokers. This allows them to sell their shares quickly if the stock goes up in price or if they need the cash. It also guarantees them safe storage. If you want to see just how safe this storage is, follow a cartload of securities from the sorting pens to the firm's vault in the basement. It takes two men working in unison to turn the wheels and dials which permit the heavy metal door to slide open. Inside, the vault is like a closet, fitted out with steel shelves and drawers in which the securities are filed. The vault in the picture on page 99 contains $500,000,000 worth of customers' stocks and bonds.

Vault Where Stocks and Bonds are Stored

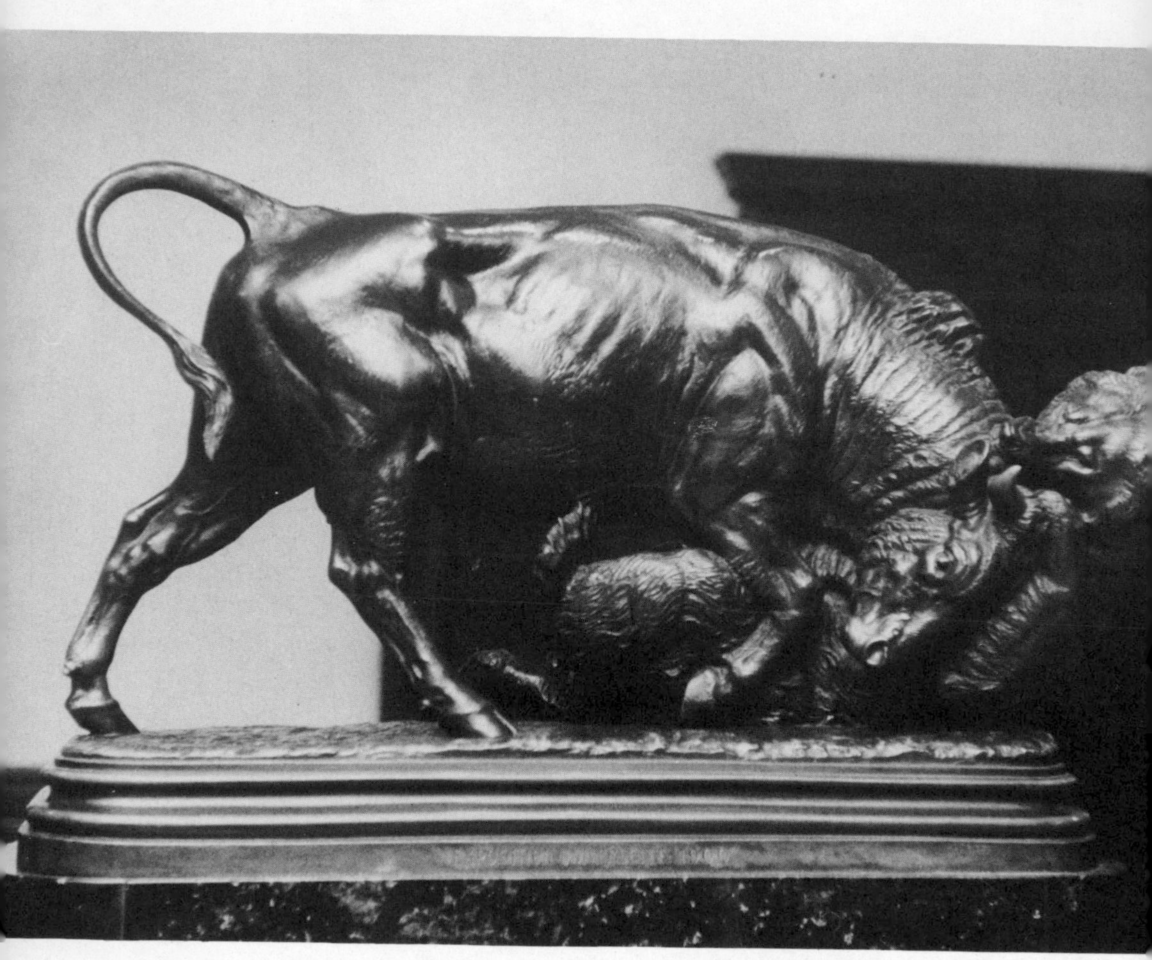

The Fight Between the Bull and the Bear

CHAPTER 8 It's not like the good old days

As you've seen, stock exchanges exist in order to provide capital for business. Men and women invest their savings in a corporation's stock. With this capital, the corporation manufactures shoes or baseball bats or television sets. It promises the investors a share of the business's profits, in the form of dividends. If the business is successful, the investor will be able to sell his stock for more money than he paid for it. This is the way it worked with Lemonade, Inc.

But there is another side to the stock market. Throughout its history the market has also been a place where men could make—and lose—great personal fortunes by speculating in stocks. The speculator is not interested in dividends. He is looking for a quick profit on his money. He buys stocks at a low price and sells them when they go up. He sells stocks at a high price and buys them when they go down. He takes a big risk for big profits—and sometimes he loses.

There have been many arguments for and against the speculator. His supporters say that he is a necessary part of a free market for capital. Without him, trading in shares would slow down. Instead of being able to buy 100 shares of Amalgamated Baseball Bat in a few minutes, you might have to wait days or weeks until you found someone who wanted to sell to you. If you were not sure of being able to buy and sell quickly, you might not invest at all. And Amalgamated Baseball Bat would then find it difficult to obtain capital for a new factory.

The gravest charges against speculators go back many years, when it was possible for a man to manipulate stock prices in order to drive them up or down. In the good old days, which might also be called the bad old days, professional traders did many things that were unethical if not downright illegal.

One sure-fire way of making money was to issue *watered stock.* The phrase originated in the cattle trade in the 1820s when unscrupulous drovers fed salt to their cows as they drove them to market. The thirsty animals drank great quantities of water just before they were weighed in at the slaughterhouse—and butchers paid as much per pound for water as they did for beef.

In the same way a promoter could buy a business for $1,000,000 and then sell $2,000,000 worth of stock in the company. One out of every two shares an investor bought was water. Sometimes the promoter was able to operate the business so efficiently that the water evaporated and the company became worth the higher capitalization. Sometimes the business failed and the investor lost his savings. But the promoter almost always prospered.

Watering stock was not limited to small, fly-by-night concerns. As the railroads crisscrossed the country, their owners made fortunes out of water. Historians report that the New York Central poured $50,000 of "absolute water" into every mile between Buffalo and New York. The Erie Railroad increased its stock from $17,000,000 to $78,000,000 in five years. Similar practices were followed by the founders of big industrial combinations. Even United States Steel, today's respected market leader, originally traded in water as well as metal. When it was organized in 1901, the value of its property was less than $700,000,000, yet its stocks and bonds, distributed to the public through the Exchange, totaled $1,402 million.

One of the professional speculator's most valuable tools was unrestrained *short selling*. Short selling means selling a stock before you own it, in the hope of being able to buy it for a lower price. Suppose you thought that the price of Amalgamated Baseball Bat was going to fall. You could ask your broker to sell 100 shares short for you at 12⅝. After making the sale, he would lend you 100 shares of the stock so that you could deliver them to the purchaser. Then, a week later, or a month later, when the price of BAT had dropped to 10⅝, you would buy

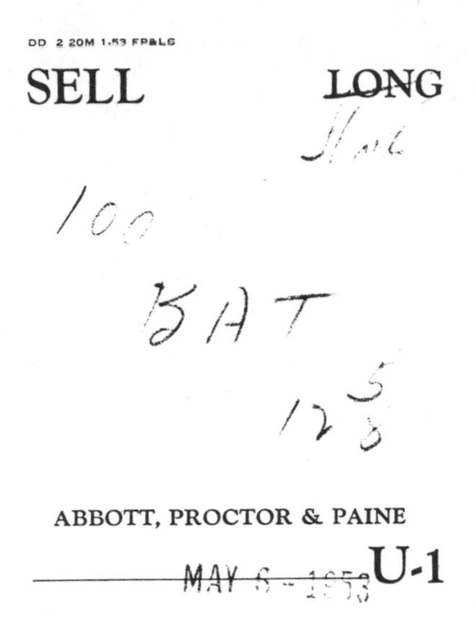

DD 2 20M 1-53 FP&LG

SELL ~~LONG~~ Short

100

BAT

12 5/8

ABBOTT, PROCTOR & PAINE

MAY 6 1953 U-1

Short Selling Order

100 shares. Because you bought for $2.00 a share less than you sold, you would have a profit of $200.

The sale of something you don't own may seem like a backward way of doing business—or even a dishonest one. Actually it has been an established practice in the securities market for centuries. If, its defenders ask, it is all right to buy a stock because you think it's going up, why not sell when you expect a drop in price? "A market in which people may buy in the hope of a rise but in which others anticipating a decline may not sell would cease to be a true market," the Stock Exchange says.

Short selling acquired a bad name because of *bear raiding*, once a popular sport of the big-time traders. A *bear* in Exchange language is a trader who expects stock prices to fall. A *bull*, on the other hand, expects a rise. You can remember which is which if you recall that a bear knocks his victim down while a bull tosses his high up in the air.

In the good old days, little was left to chance. If you were a bear—a big bear, that is—you didn't just sit around waiting for lower prices. You forced them down by any method you could think of—by rumors, deliberately created panics, and direct action.

When Daniel Drew wanted to force down the price of Harlem Railroad stock, he bribed New York's Common Council to repeal the road's franchise. The stock dropped from 100 to 72. When John W. Gates, known as "Bet-a-Million" Gates, was selling a steel stock short, he forced the closing of a number of steel mills. After the stock had fallen 30 points, the mills were opened again. The halt in production was purely a stock market maneuver.

The bears were not the only wild animals in the stock market zoo. To counter bear raids, bulls often responded with *corners*. When a big bear sold short, a big bull bought. He kept on buying until he owned every available share of the stock in which the bear was interested. When it came time for the bear to buy, so that he could return the stock he had borrowed, there was no one to buy from except the bull. The bull had a *corner on the market* and was able to set the price as high as he wished. He set it so high that the bear was ruined.

This is exactly what happened to Daniel Drew when he was raiding Harlem Railroad stock. All the time that he was selling short, Commodore Cornelius Vanderbilt was buying. The raid proceeded so rapidly that Drew and his associates did not at first realize what was happening. They continued to sell until they had sold 137,000 shares, 27,000 shares more than the company had ever issued. By then Vanderbilt owned every share of Harlem Railroad stock. After forcing the stock down to $72 a share, Drew had to settle with the Commodore at $179. It is Drew, incidentally, who is credited with the rhyme:

He who sells what isn't his'n,
Must buy it back or go to prison.

An even more famous corner was the corner in gold, engineered by Jay Gould with the assistance of Jim Fisk. Gould bought the fantastic sum of $100,000,000 in gold, forcing the price up from 130 to 160. Suddenly the government came to the rescue of the trembling short sellers with an announcement that it would sell from the federal gold reserves. The corner was smashed. In fifteen minutes gold dropped 25 points. Gould managed to sell before the price broke, but thousands of small speculators ended in bankruptcy. The government's decision to sell gold was announced on Friday, September 24, 1869, a day still known as Black Friday.

The ancient struggle between bulls and bears is dramatized in a bronze statue now standing in the lobby of the Stock Exchange Luncheon Club. The statue was commissioned by Thomas Lawson, a spectacular trader in the early years of the twentieth century. He ordered the sculptor to see that neither animal had an advantage over the other. If you will look closely at the picture on page 100, you will note that, although the bull is ready to gore the bear, the bear is braced to do an equal amount of damage to the bull.

From the Civil War until World War I much of stock market history was made by the big bulls and the big bears, colorful traders like Daniel Drew, Commodore Vanderbilt, and Jay Gould. In the 1920s the *pool* came into favor. A group of men combined forces to carry on active trading in a particular security. Pool members were usually brokers, traders, and *insiders* from the corporation whose stock was involved. The size of the pool varied from eight to as many as seventy members.

The pool operators rode prices up and down as if they were on a roller coaster. The first step was to lower the stock's price by short selling and by spreading unfavorable rumors. Step two was to buy substantial amounts of the stock at the new low price. Step three was to drive the price up and to keep it there until the pool's share could be unloaded.

No holds were barred. Publicity men planted stories about the stock's good prospects in the newspapers and on the radio. Favorable rumors were circulated as widely as unfavorable ones had been a short time earlier. As soon as the public's attention was caught, pool operators turned to *wash sales*.

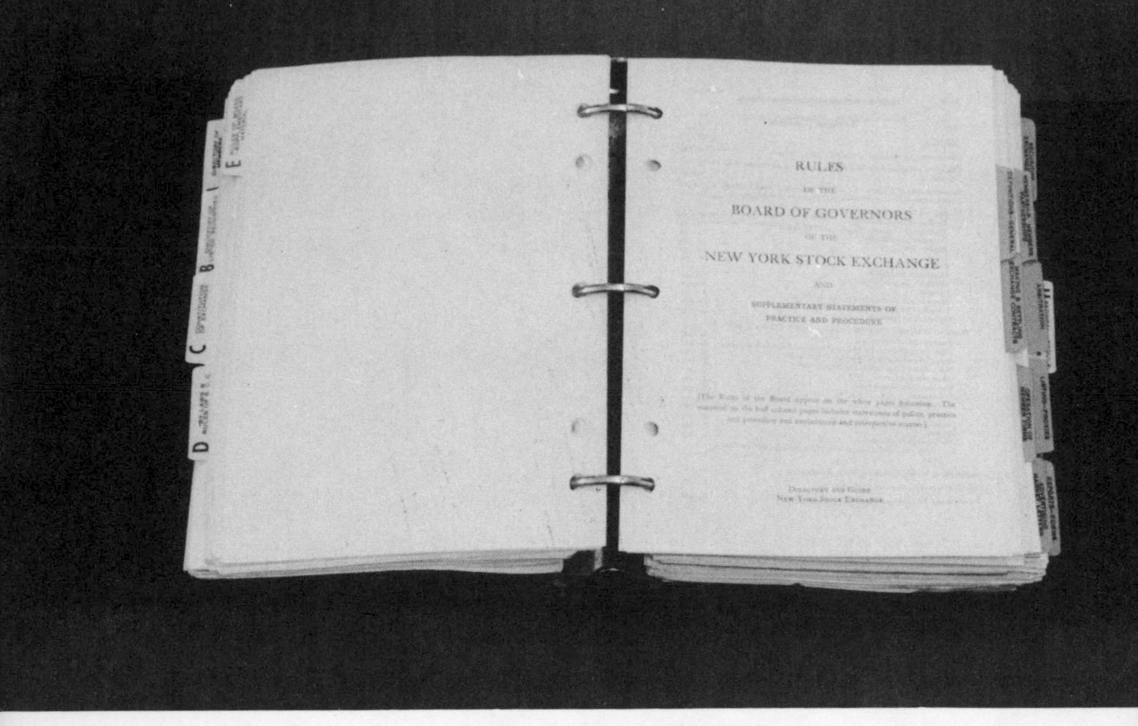

Stock Exchange Rule Book

A wash sale is a sale in which there is no real change in ownership. On Monday pool members might buy 10,000 shares of their stock through Broker X and sell 10,000 through Broker Y. On Tuesday they would sell 15,000 shares through Broker X and buy 15,000 through Y. On Wednesday they would buy 20,000 shares while their wives sold the same amount. By Thursday they were trading with their grandmothers and their great-uncles. The tape-reading public was convinced that any stocks in which there was so much activity must be "hot." By Friday the public was buying and the price of the stock quickly traveled upward.

Then came step four. The pool sold at high prices and then started the cycle all over again with short sales. To see how this operated, take a look at some figures on the Radio pool, one of the largest of the pools in the late '20s. The operators went into action on March 12, 1929. In five days Radio stock rose from 93 to 109. By the end of the month it had dropped to 80. Pool members netted $4,900,000, profiting both as bulls and bears. Only the lamb-like public lost out. In 1929 there were 105 pools in the securities listed on the New York Stock Exchange.

An encouragement to speculation was the widespread practice of buying stocks *on margin*. Buying on margin is something like buying on the installment plan—but not quite. Suppose, in the good old days, you had $100 to invest in Amalgamated Baseball Bat, then selling for $10 a share. If you bought the stock outright, paying the full cash price for it, you would be able to purchase only 10 shares. If you bought on margin, you could buy 100 shares. Your $100 would serve as down payment and your broker would loan you the balance of the money.

Unlike an installment-plan buyer, you had no intention of holding onto your stock. As soon as it went up in price to $12, you would sell. Even after paying your broker's commission and repaying his loan with interest, you would make a profit of almost $200. If you had bought outright, your profit would have been only $20.

Buying on margin worked well if stock prices went up. If. But *if* they went down, your broker asked you to increase your down payment. And *if* you were unable to do this, he could sell your stock in order to get back the money he had loaned you. This left you without your stock—and without the $100 you had originally invested.

Through margin buying, the big-time trader and the pool operator could control large blocks of stock with a small cash outlay. Their risk was slight because they also controlled the price movements in the stock. The only thing they had to fear was interference from an even bigger trader. But for the small speculator, margin buying was indeed an *iffy* business. In 1929 more than half a million men and women owned stocks on margin. When stock prices went down, not by $2.00 or $10, but $50 or $100 a share, tens of thousands of these traders saw their investments completely wiped out.

Nineteen twenty-nine has been mentioned several times in this book. Nineteen twenty-nine was the peak year of the Big Bull Market, and 1929 was the year of the Crash. Throughout the '20s, business on the stock exchanges boomed. In 1924, 282,000,000 shares were sold on the Big Board. In 1925 it was 452,000,000 shares. By 1929 the figure had grown to 1,124 million shares.

The boom was not measured by sales alone. Stock prices were rising in the same astronomical fashion. In 1923 United States Steel stock sold for $87 a share. In 1929 its price was $261. In six years American Telephone & Telegraph rose from $119.50 to $355, General Electric from $51 to $396, Radio Corporation of America from $26 to $549.

It seemed like the story of King Midas. You had only to touch a stock to see it turn to gold. All over the country people caught the get-rich-quick fever. Everyone knew someone who had just made a million in the market. Everyone had a hot tip on which stock to buy. Everyone could recite what Radio or Steel had done yesterday as easily as they could tell you Babe Ruth's batting average. Brokerage offices were jammed and the stock market made front-page headlines. Stock prices went up-up-up. Anyone warning that they might sometime go down was un-American.

But down they went. And once they started, it was like an avalanche. In September 1929 Steel sold for $261 a share. By October 24 it had dropped to $205. At the end of that day it was selling for $193. General Electric went from $400 to $315 to $283. Radio dropped 33 points, then 24 more.

October 29 was even worse. Sixteen million shares of stock were sold with prices falling an average of 40 points. The ticker was an hour and a half late in reporting sales, and member-firms stayed open all night in an effort to record the flood of sell orders. By November 13, $30,000,000,000 worth of paper profits had vanished into thin air. Between September and November, stock prices were cut almost in half.

The thirty days of September 1929 were the last of the

Board of Arbitrators

good old days. The stock market crash signaled the beginning of a depression felt around the world. Banks failed, factories shut down, and there was an army of unemployed workers and landless farmers. For a time the crisis got worse instead of better. Before it was over, many changes had taken place.

For seventeen months the Senate Committee on Banking and Currency investigated the securities market. In 12,000 pages of testimony they made public the story of promoters and pool operators, of wash sales and water. The result was the Securities Act and the Securities Exchange Act, which for the first time brought stock markets under federal control.

Today watered stock is a rarity on the organized securities market. Before a corporation issues securities, it must make a complete public statement of its financial condition to the Securities & Exchange Commission. The New York Stock Exchange's Department of Stock List, as you have read in Chapter 3, goes even further by requiring substantial assets and proven earning power before a security may be listed on the Big Board.

Short selling is rigidly controlled in order to prevent the possibility of bear raids. No sell order may cross the trading floor unless it is clearly labeled Short or Long, and short sales may be made only when a stock's price is rising. If BAT sold at 12¾ and then at 12⅞, you would be permitted to sell it short at 12⅞. If, however, the last two sales were at 13 and 12⅞, your short sale would not be allowed. The plus and minus signs on the price indicators around the trading post, shown in the picture on page 76, tell brokers when short sales may be made.

Margin buying is allowed, but the Federal Reserve Board decides what the minimum down payment must be. The Board's figure varies, depending on business conditions and the amount of margin trading. In recent years customers have been required to deposit 50 to 75 per cent of the purchase price of their stock. Today only one man in eight buys stocks on margin on the New York Stock Exchange.

The manipulation of stock prices has been made close to impossible by a series of SEC and Exchange rulings. Wash sales are outlawed. No Exchange members may participate in a pool. Corporation insiders are forbidden to sell their company's stock short. If there is an abrupt rise or fall in the price of a stock which cannot be explained by changes in the company's earnings or prospects, the SEC has a staff of tape-watchers who immediately send out investigators. Just the threat of an investigation is usually enough to stop illegal activities. Although the SEC examines some 250 market transactions each year, it seldom is obliged to punish lawbreakers.

The passage of the securities acts compelled many changes in stock market rulings, but the laws did not immediately bring about the basic reorganization of the Exchange that many people thought necessary. In Washington the chairman of the SEC said: "Exchanges have always administered their affairs in much the same manner as private clubs. For a business so vested with public interest, this traditional method

Visitors' Gallery

has become archaic." In Wall Street a battle raged between the Old Guard and the New.

The Old Guard was headed by Richard Whitney, president of the Exchange from 1930 to 1935. It was largely composed of floor traders and specialists, members who bought and sold for their own accounts. They liked their private club. Opposing them were the commission brokers, who dealt directly with the public. They were in favor of reform.

For four years the two groups fought. They set up investigating committees, prepared reports, called names. The reform group was close to winning when a dramatic incident took place. On March 8, 1938, after the gong signaled the beginning of the trading day, the president of the Exchange stepped out on the balcony overlooking the floor, the balcony shown in the picture on page 56. Quietly he announced, "Richard Whitney and Company are suspended for conduct inconsistent with just and equitable principles of trade."

Whitney's firm was bankrupt, and he had speculated with

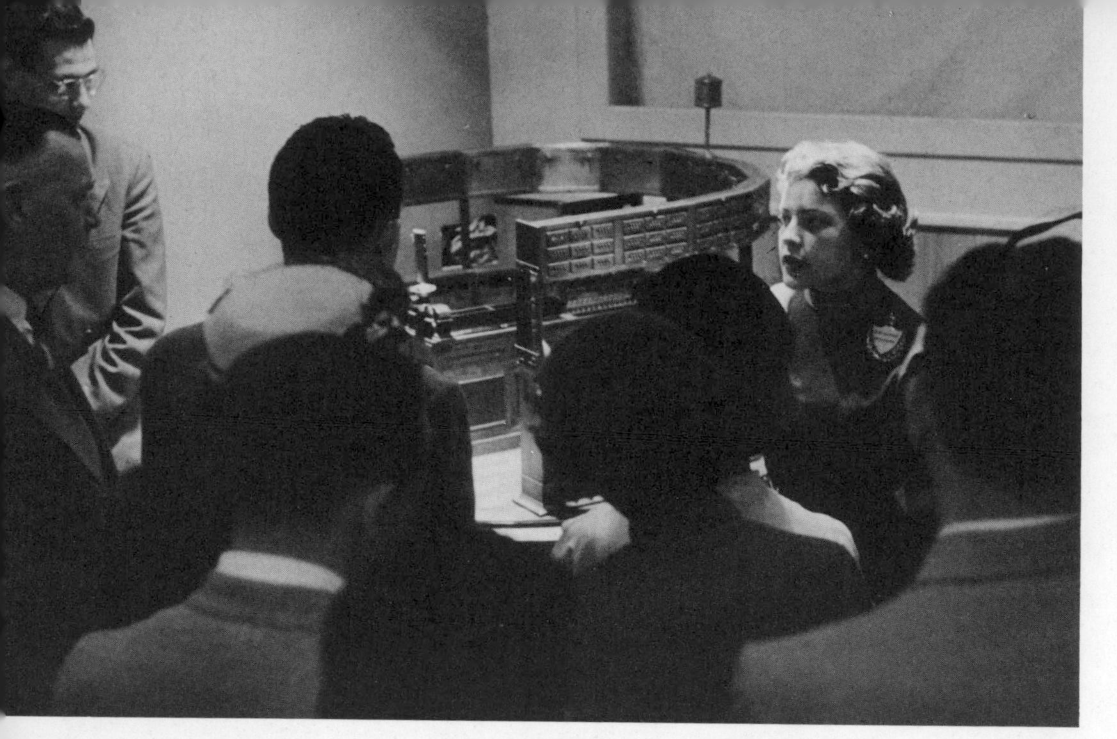

A Model of a Trading Post

securities entrusted to him for safekeeping. The leader of the Old Guard went to Sing Sing prison while the Exchange voted, by an overwhelming majority, to reorganize.

It was this reorganization that created the stock market of today, with its paid, full-time president, its broadly representative Board of Governors, and its fat book of rules. The 1,418-page rule book regulates all Exchange activities, from the behavior of members on the trading floor to the wording of their firms' advertisements. In many ways Exchange rules go beyond the SEC's in protecting the public from error or fraud.

An investor who believes that he has been unfairly treated by his broker will receive sympathy and advice from the Department of Member Firms. If the dispute cannot be settled amicably there, it is turned over to a special Board of Arbitrators. The arbitrators are Exchange members and men and women not connected with the securities business. They sit as judges, and their decision must be accepted as binding.

The picture on page 109 shows the Board of Arbitrators in session. The complainant is seated at the table in the foreground. She has charged that her broker did not obtain the best possible price when he sold some stock for her. At the next table her broker is questioning a witness. After witnesses from both sides have been heard, the Board will announce its decision. The customer is right in 25 per cent of the cases heard by the Board of Arbitrators.

In addition to this type of proceeding, the Exchange has set out to prove that it is no longer a private club, by extending a hearty welcome to the public. In the good old days you had to be a member's uncle or mother-in-law or a Very Important Person before you could visit the Exchange. Now there are crowds of sight-seers on the balcony above the trading floor and a staff of pretty guides to describe what's going on. From the Visitors' Gallery, tourists go to the Exhibit Room, where they may examine a model of a trading post and have their names printed on a piece of ticker tape.

Adjoining the exhibits is a small movie theater showing "What Makes Us Tick," a cartoon film that explains the operations of the stock market and its relation to American industry. In addition to daily showings in the Exchange buildings, "What Makes Us Tick" is projected in schools and clubs, on television and in commercial theaters.

For those who cannot travel to New York for a visit, the Exchange's Department of Public Relations has prepared a number of simply written, well-illustrated booklets, as well as *The Exchange,* a monthly magazine. Each summer, scholarships are given to professors and students in the field of business, to permit them to spend three weeks on Wall Street in an intensive study of the securities market. The American Stock Exchange co-operates in presenting this three-week course, as well as maintaining its own visitors' gallery and guided tour.

Scenes from "What Makes Us Tick"

CHAPTER 9 The stock market and you

There are 7,500,000 people in the United States today who own shares in publicly owned corporations. That's not as large a figure as it sounds if you think of it in terms of the total population. It means only 4 per cent of all U.S. men, women, and children, or one out of every fourteen adults.

You may someday choose to become the one-in-fourteen or you may swear never to buy a share of stock. Whichever decision you reach, however, should be based on facts rather than rumor. Don't buy a stock because a friend has "inside" information that it's going to go up in price. No one has "inside" information on which stocks are best buys. But everyone has available to them a considerable volume of "outside" information about general business conditions and the earnings and future plans of individual corporations.

The first place to look for facts is in your daily newspaper. Eight out of ten papers in large U.S. cities print detailed accounts of stock market activities, as well as other business and financial news. In the offices of the Associated Press in midtown Manhattan a battery of fourteen stock tickers supplies up-to-the-minute information on both the New York and American Stock Exchanges. As fast as the news comes in on the tape, it is tabulated and sent out by AP teletypes to newspapers throughout the country. In addition to the regular ticker service, the Associated Press receives reports from the New York Stock Exchange's *volume ticker,* which once an hour summarizes the total number of shares sold. Reports from the volume ticker also go to the United Press and to other New York newspapers and wire services.

Most newspapers print the information they receive from the AP in *stock tables.* The stock table looks like a printed version of the electric boards in member-firm offices. The day's report on Amalgamated Baseball Bat, for instance, might read:

1955		STOCK & DIV'D	Sls.					NET
HIGH	LOW	IN DOLLARS	100s	FIRST	HIGH	LOW	LAST	CHGE
13¼	11½	Am B Bat .70	5	12¾	13	12½	12⅞	–⅛

This tells you a number of things. In recent months the price of BAT has stayed between $11.50 and $13.25. If you'll look down the column you'll see that other stocks have a price range as much as $25. BAT's price, then, has changed comparatively little. As a general rule, stocks whose prices fluctuate widely are considered riskier investments than those with a narrow price range.

From the second column you learn that the stock has been paying an annual dividend of 70 cents a share. One hundred shares would bring a dividend of $70. You know that if you deposit money in a savings bank you will receive interest at

The Associated Press' Financial News Room

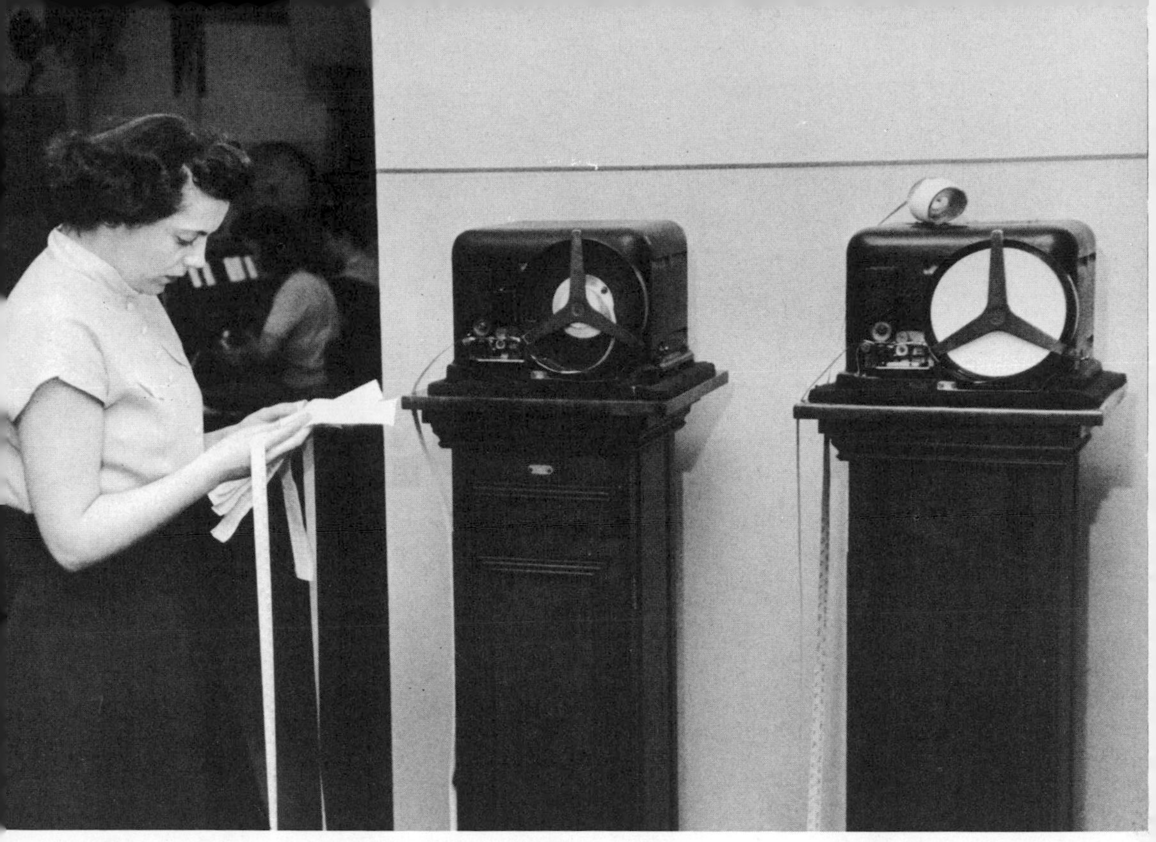

Volume Ticker

the rate of 2 or 2½ per cent. How much would an investment in BAT bring you if you bought 100 shares at 12⅝ ($1,262.50)? Five and a half per cent. This would be the *yield* on your investment. With pencil and paper and the stock table, you can easily figure out the yield of any stock listed.

Column three shows the number of BAT shares bought and sold in a day. If you compare this figure over a period of time with sales figures for other stocks, you'll know whether BAT is an active or inactive stock. A sudden increase in the number of shares traded could mean good news or bad. Perhaps people are buying because the company has just announced the invention of a plastic bat, stronger and cheaper than wooden ones. Perhaps they're selling because the new bat is a failure and the quarterly report shows a drop in profits.

The First, High, Low, and Last figures give a blow-by-blow account of BAT's selling prices for the day. The first sale was made at \$12.75, the last at \$12.87½. During trading hours it rose as high as \$13 and dropped as low as \$12.50.

The final column in the table, Net Change, compares BAT's last price yesterday and today. Yesterday, BAT closed at \$13, today at \$12.87½. The net change, therefore, was –⅛.

If you are reading a large metropolitan newspaper, you will find similar stock tables for the transactions on the American Stock Exchange, the Toronto and Montreal exchanges, and for the New York Stock Exchange's bond market. You will also notice a table titled "Over-the-Counter Securities." All securities which are not bought and sold on the exchanges are spoken of as being traded *over-the-counter*. The expression goes back to colonial days, when stocks were sold, like tea or beaver skins, over the counters of merchants or private bankers.

Banks and insurance-company stocks, government and municipal bonds are traded over the counter. So are the stocks of corporations whose businesses are too new or too small to be listed on an exchange (Lemonade, Inc., for example) and the stocks of companies whose directors, for one reason or another, do not want them listed on an exchange. The over-the-counter market is a large one—how large, no one knows exactly. But it is a safe guess that its total sales are more than the combined totals of all the exchanges.

The picture on page 119 shows the over-the-counter market at work. Suppose you place an order with the man on the right for 100 shares of Lemonade, Inc. If his firm owns shares of this stock, he will sell it to you immediately. If not, he will consult his *pink sheets* to see which dealers hold Lemonade, Inc., and at what price they are willing to sell. The pink sheets, so called because they are mimeographed on pink paper, give dealers' prices on more than 5,000 different securities.

By flipping a key on the telephone switchboard in front of him, he can speak immediately with any one of 150 over-the-counter dealers. After talking to two or three to find out who will sell for the best price, he reports back to you. If he has to

Over-the-Counter Market

pay $10 for the stock, he will sell to you for $10.50 or $11. Instead of charging a broker's commission, as Exchange members do, he makes his profit by selling the stock for a higher price than he paid for it.

Over-the-counter really means over-the-telephone. Each of the 4,000 over-the-counter firms provides its own market place. These markets are the source of capital for new business. They also offer a place where large blocks of securities can be sold, often for better prices than they would bring under the exchanges' auction-bidding system.

The over-the-counter tables in your daily paper do not list actual selling prices. The published figures are quotations, bid-and-asked prices for each security. They are furnished each afternoon by the National Association of Securities Dealers, the organization of brokers and dealers who make up the over-the-counter market.

In addition to stock tables, many daily papers publish other business and financial news. You can study reports of the production of automobiles and steel and oil, the amount of money in circulation, the number of unemployed, exports, imports, consumers' prices. You can read the latest news about individual corporations: their sales, their dividends, their *earnings.* Earnings represent a corporation's profits divided by the number of shares of stock it has outstanding. If BAT's profits for the year are $1,000,000 and there are 250,000 shares of BAT stock, BAT's earnings are $4.00 a share.

If your paper does not print this kind of information, you can turn to the *Wall Street Journal,* the Street's daily newspaper, which has a readership of 620,000. Or to the *Journal of Commerce,* another daily financial paper. Or to one of half a dozen weekly and monthly magazines in the business field. More newspapermen cover Wall Street than any other place in the United States, with the exception of Washington, D.C.

Besides the periodicals, you can consult a staggering assortment of newsletters and advisory services. Some of these publish statistics on corporation earnings, dividends, and the range of stock prices. Others offer to tell you which stocks are good investments and when to buy and sell. In the good old, bad old days, there were scores of tip sheets which "guaranteed" that the stocks they recommended would go up. Frequently they didn't, of course.

Even today the advisory services vary greatly. They range from sober analyses of business conditions to forecasts which are not far removed from fortunetelling. When the research department of a brokerage firm compiles a list of stocks with good records of dividend payments, they preface their list with a cautious reminder: "The fact that a company has paid dividends uninterruptedly for 20, 50, or 150 years is in itself no guarantee as to future payments." Contrast this with a bulletin with red-ink headlines: "I LOOK FOR A BUST IN COMMON STOCKS." The first gives you facts. The second gazes into a crystal ball.

The broad tape gives the news

Studies have been made of the accuracy of Wall Street's forecasting services. One economist presented figures to show that if you had followed the 7,500 different recommendations of the forecasters over a four-year period, you would have ended up just a little bit poorer than if you had selected stocks at random. A financial editor recently summed up a seven-year study of his own and concluded that the forecasters were wrong two thirds of the time.

The big question along Wall Street still is, "What is the market going to do?" When you read the financial news, you'll notice that the stock market is spoken of as if it were a person, an extremely agile individual with a will of his own. Stocks "push forward" or they "plummet." The market "rallies" after a "pummeling." It "eases" and "dips." It "wobbles" and "churns," "marks time," "turns soft," "dives" and "zooms." These acrobatics all refer to the general movement of stock prices. They dive down, zoom upward, or mark time by showing only slight daily changes.

But what makes these prices go up and down? Back in the '20s the Exchange was often thought of as the leader of American business. So long as stock prices rose, we had prosperity. A market decline spelled trouble. For a time the 1929 crash was blamed for the depression that followed, and stock speculation was believed the cause of all economic woes.

It was soon apparent, however, that speculation could bring ruin only to those who speculated. Instead of the fall in stock prices causing the depression, it was quite the other way around. The stock market reflects business conditions. It cannot change them.

Many people believe that stocks zoom when industrial production is on the increase and corporate profits are high. When profits are low, when unemployment is growing, then the market dives. The same thing holds true for individual stocks. When the price of steel goes up, so does the price of steel stocks. When BAT's earnings rise, that's the time to buy BAT.

This is a logical-sounding theory, but it doesn't always work. The stock market is a lopsided mirror of business conditions. Industrial production rose from 1939 to 1942 and stock prices fell. Industrial production fell for 1943 to 1946 and stock prices rose. Production was at an all-time high in 1953, yet the market wobbled and eased and sometimes plummeted. Not until the business recession of 1954 did stocks zoom again.

The theory doesn't work for individual stocks either. In 1950, Chrysler plants were closed down by a three-month strike. No Chrysler automobiles were manufactured and the company estimated its losses at more than a million dollars. But during the shutdown, Chrysler stock rose from 63⅞ to 71, its high for the year.

Stock prices are influenced by industrial production, by profits and earnings and yields. But they are also influenced by world events. Will there be a war, a cut in taxes, a depression? What will the British Prime Minister say, or the Russian Premier, or the President's economic advisers?

In Exchange circles, front-page headlines are carefully weighed. The publishers of the *Wall Street Journal* summarize news which may influence security prices and send out regular bulletins by teletype. Most member firms subscribe to this news service and in many offices it is projected on Trans-Lux screens. Customers study the *broad tape*, as the news ticker is called, with as much interest as they do the stock board.

Even in its response to news events, the acrobatic market behaves unpredictably. When the Korean War began, stock prices dropped an average of 35 points. With every rumor of peace, prices fell again. Prices rose when a Republican president was elected for the first time in twenty-four years. Prices rose also when a Republican congressman was defeated in the first political test of the new administration.

There is an explanation for these contradictions. The stock market is not a machine that responds automatically to production figures or politics. Stock prices depend on people, on the opinions of those who buy and sell shares. If investors think that a Republican administration will bring prosperity, they buy, and prices rise. If they fear that peace in Korea will touch off a depression, they sell, and prices fall.

"Emotionalism has taken the upper hand in the market,"

you'll often read in the financial news. In addition to being economists and news analysts, share owners must also be students of psychology.

The big question still is, "Will stock prices go up or down?" Perhaps it will never be answered better than it was by J. P. Morgan, Wall Street's most prominent financier from Civil War days up to World War I. Whenever he was asked, "What will the market do?" he gave the same brief reply: "It will fluctuate."

INDEX